Ylang-Ylang Socialism:
Ali Soilihi, Maoism,
and Socialist Comoros
1975-1978

Ylang-Ylang Socialism: Ali Soilihi, Maoism, and Socialist Comoros 1975-1978

by Lucas Alan Dietsche

edited by Joseph Mykut & Marie Moldovan

All rights reserved. No part of this manuscript may be reproduced or transmitted in any form or by any means, electronic or mechanical, including photocopying, recording, or any information storage and retrieval system, without prior permission in writing from I Ain't Your Marionette Press

Applications for the rights to perform, reproduce or in any other way use this content must be sent to:

mariemoldovan99@3amigosinkandsplatter.com

Published by I Ain't Your Marionette Press

P.O BOX 184

Larder Lake, ON, Canada. P0K 1L0

For orders other than individual consumers, I Ain't Your Marionette Press grants discounts on purchases of 10 or more copies of single titles for bulk use, special markets, or premium use. For further details, contact:

Sales – I Ain't Your Marionette Press

mariemoldovan99@3amigosinkandsplatter.com

Book set in Garmond

Cover Design by Joseph Mykut

Edited by Marie Dawn Moldovan and Joseph Mykut

Paperback ISBN: 978-1-998213-56-6

eBook ISBN: 978-1-998213-58-0

Tribute

Pour Guy Cidey alias Lou Belletan, alias Casimir, alias Fundi Kaji Atta, qui nous a quitté le 23 juillet 2025. Chercheur infatigable, il a consacré sa vie à restituer la vérité sur Ali Soilihi et à préserver la mémoire des Comores face à l'oubli et à la falsification. Honneur à son travail, honneur à sa mémoire.

For Guy Cidey, also known as Lou Belletan, Casimir, and Fundi Kaji Atta, who passed away on July 23, 2025. A tireless researcher, he devoted his life to restoring the truth about Ali Soilihi and to preserving the memory of the Comoros against oblivion and falsification. Honor to his work, honor to his memory.

~Kari Kweli

Foreword

The fascination sparked by the attempt at a socialist revolution in the Comoros, orchestrated by the charismatic Ali Soilihi, is the starting point of this book. Ali Soilihi's vision of transforming this archipelago into a unified, egalitarian, dynamic, independent, and expected Comorian nation stands in stark contrast to the country's current situation, marked by multidimensional crises since its independence.

Over the years, my quest to understand this revolution and its protagonists has led me to meet numerous surviving participants, and to explore the differing opinions between supporters and opponents of this movement. Even today, I continue to read various materials on this subject. I meet researchers, academics, writers, students, and journalists who have worked, written, or continue to have an interest in Ali Soilihi and the Comorian revolution. It was through this process that I came into contact with Lucas Alan Dietsche, a young doctoral candidate in philosophy. This prolonged journey through time reveals that there are still many facets of this period to uncover to better grasp this tumultuous era in the history of the Comoros.

In this work, Lucas Alan Dietsche seeks to introduce Ali Soilihi to the English-speaking world and to enshrine him in the pantheon of African revolutionaries, where his place seems strangely vacant despite his qualities as a perceptive and visionary leader. He corrects the anachronism that compares him to Thomas Sankara, asserting instead that

Sankara should be seen as the Ali Soilihi of Burkina Faso. Dietsche's approach, although clearly favorable to Ali Soilihi, is informed by a profound admiration for his leadership qualities, which, instead of personally benefiting from his position, chose to fight for collective well-being. Despite this, Dietsche does not fail to present criticisms of the Soilihi regime, thus offering a balanced overview that invites further exploration of diverse perspectives.

The book's predominantly French sources pose a translation challenge, sometimes making it difficult to capture all the subtleties of the original discourse. However, the efforts to discredit Soilihi after his death by a coup d'état seem only to have posthumously reinforced his status as an indispensable figure in Comorian and African history. Ali Soilihi remains an iconic and widely respected figure, whose impact and vision continue to resonate long after his disappearance. This book is a vibrant testimony to that.

~Kari Kweli 2024

Preface: My Journey to Socialist Comoros

Nestled in the azure waters of the western tropical Indian Ocean, the Comoros archipelago stands as a testament to the resilience and determination of its people. Despite its diminutive size, this chain of islands has seen a tumultuous history marked by coups, assassinations, and secessions. Amidst chaos, a beacon of hope appeared in the form of Comorian socialism- a movement that sought to challenge imperialist hegemony and pave the way for self-determination. Comoros, includes four islands (Swahili and French) —Ngazidja/Grande Comoros, Ndzuani/Anjouan, Mwali/Mohéli, and Maore/Mayotte—embodies the struggles of a people striving for autonomy in the face of colonial oppression. This book aims to illuminate the often-overlooked history of Comorian socialism, offering insights into its emergence, evolution, and enduring legacy.

The roots of Comorian socialism can be traced back to the colonial era, marked by exploitation and subjugation at the hands of European powers. From the imposition of foreign rule to the exploitation of natural resources, the Comorian people experienced firsthand the injustices of imperialism. It was amidst this backdrop of resistance that the seeds of socialism began to take root, offering a vision of liberation and equality.

The path to independence was fraught with challenges, as the Comorian people waged a relentless struggle against colonial forces. From nationalist revolutionary organizing, strikes, and the final vote, the fight for self-determination gained momentum, culminating in the declaration of independence in 1975. However, this newfound freedom was short-lived, as internal divisions and external interference threatened to undermine the fledgling nation.

In the wake of independence, Comoros embarked on a bold experiment in socialism, inspired by the principles of equality, justice, and solidarity. Led by the visionary leader Ali Soilihi, the socialist government implemented a series of radical reforms aimed at empowering the marginalized and transforming society. From land redistribution to education initiatives, these policies looked to build a more equitable and inclusive nation. Despite its noble aspirations, Comorian socialism faced many challenges and contradictions along the way. Internal strife, external pressures, and economic constraints threatened to derail the socialist project, exposing the fragility of revolution in a hostile world. Moreover, external attacks attested to the resolve of socialist leaders.

Though short-lived, the legacy of Comorian socialism endures as a testament to the power of collective action and the resilience of the human spirit. While the dream of a socialist archipelago may have been deferred, its ideals continue to inspire future generations in their quest for justice and equality. By reclaiming the people's history of Comoros, we can challenge hegemonic narratives and envision a world where liberation knows no bounds. The history of Comorian socialism serves as a potent reminder of the enduring struggle for freedom and justice. Despite facing formidable odds, the Comorian people refused to be silenced, their voices echoing across the sands of time. As we reflect on their legacy, let us honor their sacrifices and continue the fight for a more just and equitable world.

My interest in Comorian socialism happened with my own socialist evolutionary path. Between the years 2006-2020,

I was a member of various groups of Trotskyism. From those tumultuous years of 2006 to 2020, I was focusing mostly on issues that revolved around labor, feminist, environmental justice, transformative justice, prisoner support, and abolition in mostly rural and small towns of Minnesota and Wisconsin. Remaining a revolutionary communist and Marxist Feminist Abolitionist personally has forever changed me concentrating more on publication, propaganda, and always having the zeal of the recently converted. It was during a search for inner truth after leaving Trotskyism, I came to appreciate the works of Hegel, Nietzsche, Heidegger, New Afrikan/African socialism, Mao, Nkrumah, Cabral, anarchism, and a non-sectarian broad-based view of communism. I have never doubted that the world could be changed with revolution.

Inspiration for this book came from a work published by *Foreign Language Press* called *Like Ho Chi Minh! Like Che Guevara: The Revolutionary Left in Ethiopia*,

by Ian Scott Horst. Like Ethiopian socialism and its intent of being a part of the array of Marxist study, this book on Comoros serves to find a place in the sun. Much of the history of revolutionary Comoros, Ali Soilihi, the Secular and Social Republic of Comoros, has been cast off by bourgeois and reactionary Eurocentric writers, and/or bourgeois Comorians, and overall, as not part of international revolutionary catechism.

As a 20-year experienced revolutionary with knowledge of theory, praxis, revolutionary political grouplets and splits, history, personalities, of revolutionary communism, I am relying on my own thoughts, behaviors, and actions, and activism that comes from theoretical and praxis documentation to present a history of Comorian socialism for an English-speaking audience. For any movement in any country to overthrow capitalism comes with messy ordeals from which to learn lessons. I have always been fascinated with the on-the-ground struggle of building socialism in the most obtuse places. It was my own curiosity that I found an obsession with socialist Comoros and the personality of Ali Soilihi.

I do not claim to have all the answers or take away anything from Soilihist movements or any legacy of Ali Soilihi. I do not intend to educate Comorians on a very conflicted, ambiguous, and strained chapter of their history. I intend to allow the Western Radical Left in all its shades and hues to engage the lessons of the Social and Secular Republic of Comoros with Comorian revolutionaries on their own rules, traditions, and on their own grounds. I ask the Western Left to not look through their prism and kaleidoscope as armchair socialists or through their party positions. Fanon (1967) wrote about this as he talked to journalists and reformist socialists, of so-called Western civilization regarding:

> "You warned them: if they shed too much blood you would pretend to disown them; the same way a State- no matter which one-maintains a mob of agitators, provocateurs, and spies abroad whom it disowns once they are caught. You who are so liberal, so humane, who take the love of culture to the point of affection, you pretend to forget that you have colonies where massacres are committed in your name (Fanon,1967, lii)."

Fanon's words serve as a powerful indictment of the moral bankruptcy inherent in colonialism and imperialism, challenging us to confront the contradictions and hypocrisies that underpin systems of oppression. By shedding light on these uncomfortable truths, Fanon compels us to reevaluate our own roles and responsibilities in perpetuating or resisting injustice.

While reading the revolutionary work of Ali Soilihi, and the Social Secular Republic of Comoros, it is important to note that the revolution was made Comoros-style. Likewise, as Jose Marti regarding the Cuban revolution "The wine might be bitter, but it's ours".

I dedicate this book to EMH, Kilaika Anayejali Kwa Baruti Shakur, to the Secular and Social Republic of Comoros, to Ali Soilihi and his familiar and political descendants,

Thanks to the blog Muzdalifa House as great at promoting and displaying contemporary articles on different faucets regarding Ali Soilihi and the revolution. Thanks to the experts Lou Bellantan and Kari Kwelli through countless emails filled in the many blanks regarding various aspects of Ali Soilihi.

Methodology

I did this work without grants, or academic funding, but only because it was important for revolutionary continuity. The research relied on mostly secondary sources, English-language, or Google translatable documents, British, French, and Soilihist works. I even went to Twitter for help, tagging Comoros or anything related. For most Western readers who may not be familiar with the historical context or the country of Comoros, this text could serve as an introduction to the events and the individuals involved.

I have also contacted groups that have the mantle of "Soilihism" in vain to ask for assistance with this project. The primary and secondary documents used to distinguish between truth and fact, blog accounts, especially in languages I am not familiar with, posed a great methodological problem of which ones to admit. The many accounts of Bob Denard, the infamous warlord- pirate-mercenary-usurper of revolutions, was used to find any link between French exploitation of ylang -ylang for the infamous Chanel perfumery. Using an analogy, the part of the method was to separate the cotton from the cottonwood tree and find a very precious and peculiar seed regarding the factual information that could be gleaned.

Historiography, legends, myth, oral storytelling are all combined in deep levels of ambiguity especially when it comes to Comorian history. Journalist Samantha Weinberg wrote regarding the 1978 coup that deposed Ali Soilihi and the revolution that "I was fast coming to accept that Comorians love to tell stories, and they don't really respect the distinction between truth and fiction (Weinberg, 1994, p.45)." Journalist and Ex-Moissy member Said Hassane Jaffar writes regarding the oral tradition, of whether empiricism is exceedingly difficult to trace within Comorian's knowledge-history. Said Hassane Jaffar comments that:

> "We have to recognize that we are in the presence of a collection of rumors camped on the failings of the sacrosanct alibi of the oral tradition, outside of any bibliographical approach, outside of any undertaking to explore the mines of information which yet lie in the archives of the presidency, the various ministries, the administration in general, the army, the CNDRS (National Center for Documentation and Scientific Research), holder in particular of the *Pula Mwandeleo* (five-year plan) and especially the archives (texts and tapes) created by me at "Radio Comoros", etc. Because these archives do exist. We will talk about it again (Said Hassane Jaffar, 2003, paragraph 34)."

Jaffar's words serve as a reminder of the importance of critically evaluating historical sources and interrogating dominant narratives, particularly in contexts where oral tradition and rumors may obscure the reality of historical events. Through meticulous archival research, we can strive to uncover the complexities of the past and gain a deeper appreciation for the multifaceted nature of history.

Regarding socialist publications, I found only random links in Maoist documents in Marxist Internet Archive, and in the World Socialist Website regarding one of the contemporary coups in Comoros. With one exception, the

American communist group *Unity and Struggle* wrote a small blurb in an issue in 1976 about the revolution in Comoros.

This book contains a critique of journalism, travel writers, conservative historians, and reactionaries' slander and misconceptions of Marxism and socialism. So much harm is done using sensationalized Ripley's Believe it or Not-like stories on Africa. One example is that Weinberg (1994) records a detailed, yet sensational story called "the prince" to describe Ali Soilihi. Using questionable sources, I question the unnamed "Prince's' interview writing their view of Ali Soilihi as a "reader of cloak and dagger novels (p. 33)."

I also used many visual and audio documentaries uploaded on YouTube, recorded at the time of Ali Soilihi speaking, of Moissy marching, and agricultural projects that I could not translate due to time and resources. Curiously one YouTube video by BioGreat Tv was a simple "Biography of Ali Soilih M'tsashiwa" using cartoons to give an extremely simplistic template of the revolution. YouTube videos made by the *Foundation Mtsashiwa* were helpful with English subtitles. Many other recordings were extremely helpful of Ali Soilih himself but it was not possible to translate them. An original documentary on YouTube shows Ali Soilih in a white square cap and dashiki. The narrator says succinctly what the whole *raison d' etre* of the revolution "is happening politically and socially in this new nation deserves the greatest attention *(Djimbo la Komori,*2020)."

From YouTube, I also used songs, poems, and even fictional accounts to explain the contemporary legacy and how memory is considered regarding the revolution. The songs *"La Mort Et La Vie D" Ali Soilih* by Marginal People on their *Mémoire of a Nonperson* album, as well as Jack L'autout with his marvelous song about Soilihi were used to give analysis of contemporary support for Soilihi. A compact diskette of Ali Soilihi speeches made by Edition Coelacanthe proved great for context.

Eurocentric and pro-capitalist African research on Comoros, have taken a larger foothold stating that Ali Soilihi was a controversial "Madman of Moroni" or the so-called Pol Pot of Africa (Hugounec, 2022). Conservative historians and journals label Soilihi as the "jeans wearing anarchist". Reactionary sources continuously use citations from the revolution-usurper-king Bob Denard. Denard's own testimony regards himself overthrowing the revolution, as he found Soilihi watching porn, smoking pot with underage girls. Western radicals, write-off Comoros and its revolution if Wikipedia dictates the Comorian revolution was all about a cult of mass pillage, rape, torture, and including the use of "cistern prisons" as legacy (Walker, 2019). Furthermore, dismissing the Comorian revolution based on sensationalist descriptions found on platforms like Wikipedia does a disservice to the complexities of the historical context and the legitimate grievances that fueled the revolution. It is essential to engage with a diverse range of sources, including primary documents, scholarly analyses, and accounts from multiple perspectives, to gain a more nuanced understanding of the revolution and its legacy.

Rather than accepting simplistic portrayals of the Comorian revolution as solely characterized by violence and chaos, it is imperative to critically examine the underlying social, economic, and political factors that contributed to the uprising. This approach allows for a more comprehensive and accurate assessment of the revolution and its significance in the broader historical narrative.

Introduction

The dates of August 3, 1975, and May 13, 1978, continue to haunt the Comorian people. August 3rd was the coup that brought Ali Soilihi and the revolution to power with the help of French mercenaries. May 13th was when he was deposed by the same reactionary mercenaries. Between three years of communal councils, Red Guard-like militia and a mix of Islam and Maoism this specter forever roams the current World Bank-run Comoros.

Unknown to many international activists, communists, and revolutionaries, the events in the Comoros have escaped the attention of specifically Marxist struggles. The world's radicals have hardly paid any attention to Comorian socialism. They may because specifically either swayed by Left Eurocentrism and bourgeois propaganda and/or because of other struggles at the time received more attention. Or, because of Wikipedia writing the revolution off as so-called blood orgy of rape and violence. The Social and Secular Republic surrounded by lies, indifference, ambivalence like the East Indian Ocean surrounds the Comorian archipelago.

Ali Soilihi is not featured in the pantheon of African liberation fighters with Lumumba, Neto, Nkrumah, Cabral, Slovo, Sankara, Gaddafi, Biko, Machel, Mandela, Ben Bella, Senghor, Albert-Rene, Biko, Witney Mandela, and others. One resource indicates that Ali Soilihi is the "the Thomas Sankara of Comoros" which in fact is the reverse. Publisher and writer "Elaif M." writes on the unverified meeting of Ali

Soilihi and Sankara and the basing of socialism in Burkina Faso on socialist Comoros:

> "Another thing that often comes up is people comparing Ali to Sankara and saying that Ali was the Sankara of the Comoros. I completely disagree with that; it's a great anachronism! Ali lived before Sankara, and Sankara was inspired by Ali, not the other way around. So, it should be said that Sankara was the Ali Soilihi of Burkina Faso! It is said they met once in Madagascar when Sankara was still a young student, but this remains to be verified. What is certain is that individuals from Burkina Faso who came to the Comoros as cooperators mentioned that during Sankara's time in power, he had requested the retrieval of Ali Soilihi's archives to see what he had tried to do in the Comoros (Elair M in private conversation, 1/30/24)."

This is most import that the reciprocity and learning from different African revolutionaries was key to future and ongoing revolutionaries and it was not a one-size fit all socialism. While there are parallels between the policies and ideologies of Soilihi and Sankara, it's essential to recognize that they operated in distinct historical and geopolitical contexts. However, attributing direct influence or inspiration from Soilihi to Sankara requires careful consideration and verification of historical evidence. The purported meeting between the two in Madagascar and Sankara's alleged interest in Soilihi's archives may shed light on potential connections between their respective agendas.

Ultimately, whether Sankara was directly influenced by Soilihi or not, both figures left indelible marks on the history of their respective countries and the broader African continent. Their legacies continue to inspire movements for social justice, equality, and self-determination across Africa and beyond.

Ali Soilihi remains to this day, the "Mongozi " (*the Guide* in Swahili). Like Sankara, Soilihi tried to fight to break the chains of French imperialism on Comorian conditions and traditions. The book will try to educate Western Marxists on the Comorian revolution. Sartre said in the 1970s and still true today in Fanon's preface regarding Western Marxism:

> "The metropolitan Left is in a quandary: it is well aware of the true fate of the "natives," the pitiless oppression they are subjected to, and does not condemn their revolt, knowing that we did everything to provoke it. But even so, it thinks, there are limits: these guerrillas should make every effort to show some chivalry; this would be the best way of proving they are men. Sometimes the Left berates them saying: "You're going too far; we cannot support you any longer." They don't care a shit for its support; it can shove it up its ass for what it's worth. As soon as the war began, they realized the harsh truth: we are all equally as good as each other. We

have all taken advantage of them, they have nothing to prove, they won't give anyone preferential treatment. A single duty, a single objective: drive out colonialism by every means. And the most liberal among us would be prepared to accept this, at a pinch, but they cannot help seeing in this trial of strength a perfectly inhuman method used by subhuman to claim for themselves a charter for humanity: let them acquire it as quickly as possible, but in order to merit it, let them use nonviolent methods (Sartre cited in Fanon, 1967,p.xxi)."

"The attitude of the "Metropolitan Left" towards revolutionary movements in colonized or oppressed regions presents the Left may sympathize with the plight of the oppressed and understand the reasons behind their revolt but still expects them to adhere to certain standards of conduct or "chivalry" in their struggle for liberation."

"The revolutionaries the revolutionaries recognize the inherent equality among themselves and their oppressors, regardless of any superficial distinctions. They view the struggle against colonialism as their singular duty and objective, with nonviolent methods "being seen as a luxury that they cannot afford in their quest for liberation.

This highlights the tension between the expectations of the metropolitan Left and the uncompromising resolve of revolutionary movements in the face of colonial oppression. It challenges the notion that revolutionaries must conform to certain standards or methods deemed acceptable by external observers, emphasizing instead the urgency and necessity of their struggle for freedom and dignity.

Comoros waged its revolution in the conditions presented on its own terms. The creation for nationalism and a nation-state that was independent from France, Soilihist socialism came in at stages. These stages happened because of how Comoros was economically developed. Firstly, as a European fresh water stop, to trade center, and then as an endless well of cash crops. Like all African revolutionary movements coming into conflict with feudal-bourgeois relations and quickly breaking from fabrics of centuries of colonial rule, many were being led by anti-imperialist, socialist nationalist group, and personalities (Walker, 2007). Like many independences struggles on mainland Africa trying to overcome centuries of Eurocentrism, racism, colonialism, race, and dialect division, this also happened regarding amongst the Comorian islands. At most it is better to have three years of socialism than the most progressive Comorian capitalism.

Regarding a healthy class-conscious analysis regarding Ali Soilihi, the revolution, and proper historiography, future reactionary ambassador of Comoros, Eliphas G. Mukonoweshuro (1990) contends that book is yet to be written and that

> "We are still waiting for our researchers, our scientists, our historians, our sociologists and our journalists to offer us the opportunity to rightly appreciate what can be retained by the collective memory of the period 1975-1978. But while waiting for the time to read it again, we already know that

> Ali Soilih has distinguished himself by the fierce desire to oblige the Comorians to know how to rely first on themselves and to negotiate the interdependencies necessary for their evolution towards a global development system on a human scale (Mukonoweshuro,1990, p. 56)."

This reflects a call for further research and analysis by various experts—researchers, scientists, historians, sociologists, and journalists—regarding the period from 1975 to 1978, particularly concerning the legacy of Ali Soilih in Comoros during his presidency.

This allows us to appreciate the events and developments of that time, which may have a significant impact on the collective memory of the Comorian people. The implies that the historical significance of this period has not been fully understood or properly documented, hence the call for further investigation.

Mukonoweshuro (1990) highlights a positive aspect of Ali Soilihi's presidency, noting his strong emphasis on self-reliance and the negotiation of interdependencies for the advancement of Comoros. It suggests that Soilihi sought to steer the country towards a development model that prioritized the well-being and empowerment of its citizens on a human scale, rather than relying solely on external influences.

This work on Comorian revolution regards itself as only a primer in socialist theory and history of Comorian revolution. This book does not lay claim to be the book Mukonoweshuro wants to have, but to introduce Comorian socialism to the "metropolitan left" and to counter bourgeoisie narratives.

Mao writes regarding class-conscious writing and ideology that:

> "[p]roletarian ideology arises from the class struggle in bourgeois society. We should therefore understand that while bourgeois ideology is dominant, proletarian ideology also exists, secondarily, alongside it" (Mao, 1961, p. 23). Mao urges that although bourgeois ideology dominates under capitalism, proletarian ideology simultaneously emerges from class struggle and persists in a secondary position, preparing the grounds for revolutionary transformation.
>
> The Foundation Maschiwasa, a non-profit that carries the picture of Soilihi and fosters understanding for socialist Comoros, writes that "let history be the only judge" (Foundation Maschiwasa, 2018, para. 1).

This book is proletarian combat literature to present only three years of Comoros history—it was independent, sovereign, a workers and peasant democracy. To create socialism under the eyes of atrophic French colonization, the guns of Bob Denard, and the chauvinist conservative attitudes of an archipelago country that had to break from feudalism, bourgeoisie attitudes would be overwhelming.

So, without further ado, I introduce the Western Marxist world to the Social and Secular Republic of Comoros, Ali Soilihi and the revolution that came out of the gun. If another case study is needed for to prove the oppression of a small African country by a white supremacist power, and how that small archipelago achieved a socialism by rights, and finally how a mercenary can continue to ruin that countries' destiny it is Comoros.

~Stay Dangerous, Lucas Alan Dietsche, Year 5 (2025)

Notes on Comorian Names and Language

This work relies on mostly primary and secondary documents as well as tertiary media and blogs that underwent a Marxist analysis of polemics and dialectics. There are many different spellings regarding French, Swahili, and Shikomori languages. This came to a momentous task regarding specifically the spelling of names of Soilihi and/or Saleh and/or Swahili. In many instances using primary sources, I cite the whole name. Also, to stop the othering non-Western language words, I do not italicize Swahili or Shikomori words.

In this research I have found that there are three spellings of Ali Soilihi, and/or Saleh, and/or Soilih. I refrain from changing whichever version in the first-person citation but use the "Soilihi" version since that is the version on his tombstone. There is also a version of "Moissy" and "Mwassi." For this I used the commonly held version of "Moissy."

Table of Contents

Tribute _____ v

Foreword _____ vi

Preface: My Journey to Socialist Comoros _____ viii

Methodology _____ xiii

Introduction _____ xvii

Notes on Comorian Names and Language _____ xxv

Early Feudal History of the Misnamed Islands of the Moon _____ 29

Independence Birth Pangs: Creation of a Nation Without a State _____ 36

    Independence from Afar _____ 37

    Molinaco in Tanzania _____ 40

    MOLINACO in Madagascar _____ 49

    Greens, Whites, and Reds on the Archipelago _____ 56

Enter The Mongozi: Ali Soilihi _____ 60

    Time to liberate Maore? _____ 64

    Abdallah Regime and Independence _____ 68

Coup d' Ali Soilihi _____ 70

    Pink March to Liberate Maore! _____ 85

Socialist Revolution, Mongozi Ali Soilihi, and the Social and Secular Republic _____ 89

    Religion and Sorcery _____ 98

Archipelago-Unity and the Creation of the Nation-State 101

Propaganda for the Masses _____ 104

Revolutionary Education Schools and Literacy Campaign
_____ 111

Language of Ideology _____ 114

Youth and Revolutionary Art _____ 120

Power to the Mourdiyas! _____ 124

Days of Ylang-Ylang Socialism _____ *128*

The Grande Marriages and the liberation of Gender ___ 132

Defending the Revolution _____ 135

Moissy, and the Republic of the Young People _____ 141

Soilihism and Internationalism _____ 152

People's Republic of China _____ 155

Seychelles _____ 157

Democratic People's Republic of Korea _____ 158

Triple Trouble: Madagascar Massacres, Mountain
Explosions, and Iconi _____ *160*

Majunga Rataka _____ 160

Karthala _____ 165

Iconi _____ *167*

Returning From the   Point of no Return _ 173

Then Came a Pirate and His Black Dog _____ 178

Bellatan Version _____ 184

Hebditch and Connor Version _____ 187

Time Magazines Version _____ 187

Lamb's Version _____ 189
Masawai Version _____ 190
Post-Mortems and Myths _____ *201*
Legacy of Mongozi _____ 203
My Soilihism is Better than Yours: Elainou vs. Hassan Jaffar _____ 212
Cisterns Legacy is Not Just for Water Anymore, Example in Oral Tradition _____ 217
Theory of Soilihism _____ *224*
Short Epilogue: Maore/Mayotte _____ *232*
Appendix A _____ *233*
Appendix B: Constitution of the Social and Secular Republic of Comoros _____ *240*
Appendix C: Snippets from the Documentary La Reform Araire by Bambao Radio Télévision (BRTV) _____ *255*
Bibliography _____ *259*
Index _____ *268*
Biographies _____ *270*
Author _____ 270
Editors _____ 271
Suggested Reads _____ **273**

Early Feudal History of the Misnamed Islands of the Moon

A key linguistic reference to the naming of the Comorian islands is that the "Comoros Islands" is not the same as "Comoro Island" ending in 's'. In English, the area is known as "the Comoro Islands" or simply, "the Comoros". The Comoro Islands was an earlier settlement that included Zanzibar and other coastal towns that did not survive into French control. The name later became the Comoros Islands or collectively known as the Comoros.

Another error is the Comoros being called "the islands of the moon". This is a mistake due to a misinterpretation of a label on a 12th-century map drawn by the Arab geographer al-Idrisi. The label is written in Arabic and correctly identifies the islands—the Arabic meaning of 'al Qmr' is "the moon." Writers unfamiliar with the islands misunderstood the label and published the name as "islands **A Feast for Vampires** " (Ottenheimer, 1994).

This misinterpretation likely led to the islands being referred to by this incorrect name in subsequent writings and maps. It illustrates how errors in translation or understanding can perpetuate misconceptions over time, highlighting the importance of accurate interpretation and contextual knowledge when studying historical texts and maps.

The early settlement to the Comoros Islands is connected to pre-Islamic myths. Comoros' chronology of pre-Islamic settlement is, like the misnomer of being the Islands of the Moon. Legend has it a djinn drops a jewel, which forms a great circular-shaped inferno. What came was the Karthala volcano and the creation of the largest of the island of Ngazidja/Grande Comoros.

The geography of Ptolemy and the journey of the Eritrean Sea also refer to this part of the world. Ibouroi Ali Tabibou, interviewed by Keri (2018), states specifically that the history of Maoroe/Mayotte confirms the Bantus spoke around the islands before Persian migration. As for the history of the settlement of Maore/Mayotte, research confirms that the Bantu speakers' archaeological work still cannot confirm for sure previous migrations and authentic Bantu travel.

There is discrepancy regarding human settlement of the Comoros around the 1600s, and the rise of sugar cane plantation economies increased the use of chattel slavery (Keri 2008). This highlights the role of sugar cane plantation economies in the region and how they contributed to the expansion of chattel slavery. This suggests that the demand for labor in the sugar cane industry led to the increased use of enslaved individuals as chattel in the Comoros.

Early traders, and later capitalists drew an interest in Comoros as a place for potable water and commodities. Starting in the 10th century, migrants from the Arab area brought chattel slavery to Maore/Mayotte and later everywhere in the archipelago.

Arabian navigator, Ibn Majid, noted in the 15th century that the city of Domini on the island of Ndzuani/Anjouan was a major port for African, Indian, and Persian sailing vessels. Merchants sailed between the Comoros and ports in Africa, Arabia, and southern Asia trading in a wide variety of goods that included rare gems, exotic animals, woods, cloths, slaves, ambergris, and spices.

Because of this forced introduction of ylang-ylang and other perfume plants by French and Arab merchants to grow on the archipelago, the Comoros would be known as the "Perfume Islands" to exploiters (Walker, 2019). The term "Perfume Islands" for the Comoros became associated with the production of fragrances due to the cultivation of ylang-ylang and other perfume plants. This association may have been exploited by colonial powers or other exploiters for economic gain or marketing purposes.

This aggravating creation of class conflict of feudalism and later capitalism in Comoros, stemmed from uneven developmental causality. The absence of substantial nationalist or progressive bourgeoisie and the impossibility of an independent capitalist development militates against the future existence of bourgeois democracy i.e., even in its restricted form. What exists is a caricature of bourgeois democracy that takes the limitations of virtual excesses and, instead, establishes an all-embracing authoritarian rule (Alemayehu,2006). Ottenheimer and Ottenheimer (1994) discuss the grandiose personalities of the French bourgeoisie:

> "[t]wo personalities dictated an imperialist bourgeoisie in the classical French sense and the national bourgeoisie in Comoros. Sultan Said Ali was seeking domination over Ngazidja and appealed to French imperialism to support his claims. Leon Humblot, a museum director in Paris and soon-to-be French capitalist established

> plantations to produce essential oils. Humblot assisted Said Ali in deposing the last ruling sultan of Ngazidja, Sultan Hachim. The Humblot Company (Societete Humblot or Societe Anoyme de la Grande Comoroe). In 1889 Humboldt was made Resident over Ngazidja. By 1893 the company controlled more than half of the islands land area and owned several company towns and indentured slaves. In 1914 he died after being sued by Sultan Said Ali for compensation and control of the Humboldt Society (*Ottenheimer &Ottenheimer*, 1994, p. 24)."

Sultan Said Ali sought domination over Ngazidja/Grande Comore and allied with French imperialism to support his claims.

On the other hand, Leon Humblot, a French capitalist and museum director in Paris, established plantations in Comoros to produce essential oils, notably from ylang-ylang and other perfume plants. Humblot's collaboration with Sultan Said Ali included assisting him in depositing the last ruling sultan of Ngazidja, Sultan Hachim.

Subsequently, Humblot's company, the Humblot Company (Société Humblot or Société Anonyme de la Grande Comore), became influential in the region. In 1889, Humblot was appointed Resident over Ngazidja, granting him significant control over the island.

By 1893, Humblot's company controlled more than half of the island's land area and owned several company towns, utilizing indentured labor, which is mentioned as "indentured slaves" in the passage.

Between the 1600-1900's British, American, and French ships used the Comoros specifically the island of Ndzuani/Anjouran to refresh potable water supplies and food stuffs. Using the islands quickly changed between wayside stop and a place for spice monoculture. Ships were built larger, and the Comoros islands were no longer needed to refresh supplies, when the Suez Canal was created. The Comoros was no longer a part of maritime trade as capitalism created new forms of oppression for the islands. In the section called "A Feast for Vampires" Horst (2020) writes regarding Africa as whole, but can be said the same for Comoros:

> "For centuries Europe, joined later by the United States of America, has treated Africa as a mind of miraculously bottomless well out of which it could draw an endless supply of resources for the construction of its own wealthy, modern societies, with ultimately very little concern for what the draining of that well meant for Africa itself-or its population (p.366)."

The historical relationship between Europe, later joined by the United States, and Africa, characterizing it as exploitative and one-sided. It suggests that European and American powers have treated Africa as a source of endless resources to fuel their own wealth and development, without much consideration for the consequences for Africa or its people.

The metaphor of Africa being seen as a "bottomless well" implies that European and American powers viewed the continent as a boundless reservoir of natural wealth that could be exploited indefinitely. This exploitation is depicted as draining the well, suggesting that Africa's resources were extracted without regard for their finite nature or the long-term impact on the continent's environment, economy, and population.

Horst (2020) continues discussing Eurocentrism and Leninism, noting that in the post-colonial era, those who found Lenin's economic insights too Eurocentric have coupled them with Frantz Fanon's exploration of the psychologically brutal effects of colonial exploitation and oppression. This synthesis offers a more complete understanding of the devastation imperialism leaves in its wake (Horst, 2020, p. 367).

To fight early French imperialist incursions, there is only a slight mention of a rebellion in 1891 by enslaved people in Nzwani, which resulted in the sacking of Domoni by French troops (Ottenheimer & Ottenheimer, 1994). This rebellion reflects the resistance of enslaved people to French colonization and their efforts to challenge the imposition of colonial rule. The sacking of Domoni by French troops was a violent suppression of the rebellion and underscores the asymmetrical power dynamics between the colonizers and the colonized.

After the Berlin Conference of 1886, European imperialism divided Africa into spheres of influence, and the Comoros became part of Francophone imperialism. The French bourgeoisie aimed to dissuade Portuguese capitalism in spices and British dominance in maritime trade. France deliberately divided sultan clans using sultanate and feudal norms to maintain inter-sultan hostility.

Comoros was subsequently declared a French colony in 1912 and later designated an Overseas Territory in 1946. Civil service and educational opportunities were then made available in Madagascar and Paris.

French and Arab landowners ensured that the oppressed masses in Comoros were exploited for ylang-ylang and vanilla production. A young Ali Soilihi was intricately woven into this French overseas territory and the post–World War II economy.

Independence Birth Pangs: Creation of a Nation Without a State

As written in Walter Rodney's *How Europe Undeveloped Africa* (2008), Comoros was part of the wide network of "overseas Frenchmen" of French colonial interests. French imperialists kept Comoros a plantation-based monoculture economy, exporting one-third of products.

Most manufacturing and/or heavy industry were wood and metal workshops, soft drink plants, and factories for the sole processing of copra, ylang-ylang, and vanilla that only France exported.

Being on an active volcanic site near Mount Karthala, the only mineral which was in use was pozzolana, a volcanic ash used for making cement.

Before independence, the most oppressed were the wage-farmers, leaving semi-proletarians and proletarians left to be a minority. This would later reinforce Maoist philosophy on the emphasis on the peasantry as the vanguard of revolution in colonial underdeveloped countries of the Global South.

At time of independence, Comorian total population was about 250,000 while either peasants or proletarians were about 135,639. From this population only 13,000 were proletarians, with about 2,699 in the public sector and about 10,611 in the private sector (Roberts, 2021).

This data offers insight into the distribution of labor within the Comorian population, highlighting the relatively small proportion of proletarians compared to the total population and the predominance of agricultural activities (represented by the peasants) in the economy. Additionally, it underscores the division between public and private sector employment among proletarians, indicating the presence of both state-controlled and privately-owned enterprises in the economy.

The islands possessed virtually nothing in the way of infrastructure necessary for any sort of independent bourgeoisie development. For roads, there were only 750 kilometers, but only four hundred kilometers of them were perennially passable. Seaports were unable to accommodate all sizes of commercial, public, and private shipping. Air Comoros was barely beginning as a French-owned passenger airline. Imports were only up to 30,000 tons of rice. Other infrastructure, including the commercial fishing fleet, was virtually incipient (Walker, 2019).

The challenges posed by inadequate infrastructure in the Comoros Islands likely hampered economic development and the emergence of an independent bourgeoisie. Addressing these infrastructure deficiencies would be crucial for fostering economic growth and improving living standards in the region.

Independence from Afar

Many Comorian experts and scholar at the time, mentioned that was hardly anything pre-1975 resembling mass independence movements of Comoros:

> "There were no mass movements articulating the politics of dissent or galvanizing anti-colonial agitation. No nationalist movement, even of the most syncretic type developed and, consequently, no 'insurgent' nationalist ideology capable of giving a national identity and defined national goals emerged. With the highest illiteracy and mortality rates in Africa and one of the lowest per capita incomes in the world, the Comoros simply did not offer the necessary 'raw material' for mass-based nationalist politics. Consequently, political parties were simply organized cartels for elite intrigues to capture the extremely meager spoils of office (Mukonoweshuro,1990, p.559)."

This paints a picture of a politically and socially fragmented society in the Comoros, characterized by a lack of mass-based nationalist politics and the dominance of elite interests in shaping political dynamics. It underscores the complex interplay of socio-economic factors, colonial legacies, and political structures in shaping the historical trajectory of the Comoros Islands.

Because of this vacuum of independence movements, in July 1963 M. A. Al-Fassy wrote to French President Charles de Gaulle laying out what would become part of the Comorian independence movement:

> "As I am a Comorian [sic] youth by birth and a nationalist by nature of love to my country and her people,' he began, 'I would like to express my independent views and version of the trend on which our beloved country is now drifting at this juncture [sic] of the changing wind on the African continent."

Like many, Al-Fassy wanted nationalism and independence to include the Comoros (Roberts, 2021, p. 412)." This captures the spirit of nationalism and aspirations for independence among Comorian youth, highlighting their desire to shape the future trajectory of their country in alignment with their own values and aspirations.

Comorian nationalism struggles resulted in organizers pushing for independence from abroad in other anti-colonialist states and/or within the belly of the beast of France itself. These places were created for exiled activists to engage with activated groups.

But unlike many exiles that had to migrate from areas because of political repression, Comorian exiles like Ali Soilihi moved to Tanzania or Madagascar, France, or other Francophonic spheres because of vocational and educational opportunities (Roberts, 2021).

Feelings of nationalism were conflated. One sailor at the time said, "I was proud to be Comorian, although I had no particular love for the country. At that time, it was above all the Comorians who interested me, much more than the Comoros" (Kweli, 2018, para. 8).

Comorians either had no sense of nationalism or had a sense of nationalist activism that could be united with other groups on the archipelago.

Molinaco in Tanzania

One of the countries to have Comorians fight for Comorian independence was in Tanganyika. Tanganyika had gained its independence from Britain in 1961 and soon adopted a government based on "African socialism."

Zanzibar, another longtime British colony, became independent in 1963 and overthrew the ruling Arab elite in a violent revolution the following year. The island state then merged with Tanganyika to form the new nation of Tanzania.

This is where one of the larger organizations based their work on. The National Liberation Movement of Comoros (Mouvement de libération nationale des Comores, or MOLINACO) was one of the many grouplets that contested through their wanted legitimacy to contest the French bourgeoisie, Comorian bourgeois, and be accepted by leaders of African revolutionaries, local non-MOLINACO, and other Comorian exiles by being in Zanzibar and Tanganyika.

Like other Francophonic African liberation movements, MOLINACO demanded self-determination and independence.

What would be a defined shift in the Comorian revolution was the language regarding elders and youth. Shikomori-speaking Comorians (wageni) were confined to older generations and younger Zanzibar-born Comorians (wazalia).

There is much information regarding the non-activist or independence movement regarding the Comorian diaspora in other parts of continental Africa. Comorians in primarily Kenya, Tanganyika, and Zanzibar claiming the status of 'non-native' to access commercial and legal rights and protections.

Tensions between the different islands and generation-speaking did not help creating the sense of Comorian community specifically in Madagascar, leading to a divided culture of nationalism.

Before engaging in propaganda against French imperialism, Comorian nationalist elements worked within existing groups in Zanzibar, Tanzania, and Madagascar. One such existence was the Comorian Associations. Networks of Comorian Associations connected Comorians all over continental Africa.

Almost all Comorians inhabiting Zanzibar were either from the islands Ngazidja and Ndzuani, but not from Maore/Mayotte. In Tanganyika, the Comorian nationalist community was split in its politics, and many were activists of the Tanganyika African National Union (TANU). Comorian Association leaders who supported Comorian non-nativity backed the United Tanganyika Party, of which multiracialism was considered ridiculous by TANU.

Specifically in Zanzibar, Comorian communities became part of the problem of racialism. Because of these amphibious divides, the Zanzibar Nationalist Party (ZNP) was made up of the local Arab ruling classes. The ZNP competed for power with the Afro-Shirazi Party (ASP), whose tradition was based on capitalism and racism as a means to activate the 'African' populations (Robert, 2021).

This highlights the complex political dynamics in Zanzibar, characterized by competition between nationalist and capitalist-oriented parties, as well as efforts to mobilize different segments of the population along racial or ethnic lines.

Let me know if you'd like help applying this structure across more sections or formatting your references for APA. I can also help you build a style sheet to keep everything consistent.

At the Inter-Territorial Conference of the Comorian Associations in Zanzibar in the spring of 1960, representatives for the conference reinserted that obstacle regarding Comorian involvement in the progression of these countries be rejected. Yet, the conference gave the green light for Comorians to take part in politics in Zanzibar. The ASP was very ambivalent towards Comorian personhood in Tanzania because of its "African" side of its identity but still pushed for votes and Comorian participation. Both Tanzania/Zanzibar and Madagascar in many ways used Comorian activists' means to their own ends.

So incredulous was this anti-Comorian line regarding Comorians that the ASP assaulted the African National Congress (ANC) of Tanganyika. This party was based on racialism, to create the publicity secretary post for a Comorian named Kaikai Saïd Kaikai, as its publicity secretary. In Roberts (2021), an ASP supporter wrote to an ANC leader that 'in Zanzibar there is not even one Comorian who accepts being called an African and the same is true across all East Africa.' Many Comorians supported ASP as a connected multi-ethnic African nationalist group and were required to support African identity.

Regarding the hegemonic divisiveness between ethnic groups, TANU's Bibi Titi Mohammed told ASP that the press had told Comorians not to come to Zanzibar. Dissuasion of Bibi's claim regarding Comorian identity was told to Bibi that "this man is a Comorian and in Tanganyika there are thousands of Comorians, so what should we do with them?" Bibi Titi Mohammed's response was "I think this man has forgotten that he is an African."

This continued the racism against Arabs as pro-slave "bloodsuckers." Bibi Titi, with the same voice, tried to get Comorians to vote for the TANU to stop Arab discrimination against them. More propaganda from the TANU said that the Comorians are "selfish people" and do not put their Africanity first and support the ZNP.

This ethnic ambiguity constrained how to create united front work and allies to forward the cause of Comorian independence. Both parties were hostile to Comorians, but both preyed on their Arab and African sympathies (Walker, 2020).

Both political parties mentioned are described as hostile to Comorians. Despite this hostility, the parties are said to have preyed on the Arab and African sympathies of the population. This implies that they may have exploited ethnic or racial divisions within Comorian society for their own political gain.

In 1961, in Moroni, a Chamber of Deputies took internal control over Comorian affairs. The President of Governors came under the control of an ex-deputy of Comoros in the National Assembly in Paris, Saïd Mohamed Cheikh. Under this new reformist power scheme, many bourgeois nationalist leaders wanted more autonomy as Africans pushed their own respective countries' liberation.

A national flag, national anthem, and at least representation in the diplomatic field for the Comoros were negated by De Gaulle. De Gaulle attacked Saïd Mohamed Cheikh, saying that French aid would end with independence and the islands were continuously given a classification of "overseas territory" (Walker, 2020).

The political pressure exerted by France on Comoros in the context of the struggle for independence underscores the challenges faced by Comorian leaders like Saïd Mohamed Cheikh in navigating the complexities of colonialism and asserting their aspirations for self-determination.

This negligence of Comoros independence by France finally led up to the formation of MOLINACO to put Comorian independence on the agenda. Experiences of the Comorian diaspora regarding reformist political sovereignty gave them more reason to exalt radical ideas for an anti-colonial struggle. Ex-ASP Comorian supporters, dissenters of the archipelago, and students, with the help of a teacher from Nzazidja/Grande Comoros helped secretly form MOLINACO in May of 1962. Zanzibar was still under British empire rule, so MOLINACO tried to get Comorian members of TANU on board.

To find like-minded revolutionaries and shore up a full-on struggle for independence and decolonialization, MOLINACO attended the Afro-Asian People's Solidarity Conference in Tanganyika, in February 1963. MOLINACO leaders told the conference that a nationalist group had been created and that MOLINACO was the legitimate group for Comoros independence. MOLINACO had been working towards independence "in the name of the Comorian people living in the Comoros archipelago and in other countries around the world" in a struggle for "total and unconditional independence" (Roberts, 2021).

Instead of acknowledging ZNP's message of solidarity for MOLINACO, the leaders rejected it. MOLINACO made sure conference attendees knew that ZNP blocked the Comorian liberation movement through reactionary racialist divisiveness. Going further than that, MOLINACO's statement incurred Zanzibar's racialism by saying, "We warn the Arabs in Zanzibar to refrain from interfering in the affairs of Comoro Islands, we know how much they have done and are still doing to oppress the Africans of Comoros in various fields and walks of life" (Roberts, 2021, p. 34).

At the foundation of the Organization of African Unity (OAU), MOLINACO pushed for support from Egypt, the People's Republic of China, and the USSR. Infighting occurred when some members of MOLINACO tried appealing to France by pushing a more moderate line (Roberts, 2021).

The internal dynamics and strategic debates within the Comorian independence movement, particularly within organizations like MOLINACO, underscore the complexities and challenges involved in navigating the path to independence, including differing perspectives on tactics, alliances, and engagement with colonial powers.

Even though MOLINACO claimed to be a legitimate independence movement, they did not have legitimacy to many archipelago Comorians. More internal and external constraints resulted in MOLINACO's early birth pangs resulting in their disconnectedness to the daily life on the ground to the archipelago. Leaders in OAU and Tanganyika's foreign minister attacked the incipient group because as per MOLINACO opponents, MOLINACO did not have Comorians on the archipelago and/or that MOLINACO were effective organizers. This had all changed by the Afro-Shirazi Youth league overthrow the ZNP government, united by members of the UMMA Party, and part-Comorian activist Abdulrahman Mohamed Babu.

Abdulrahman Mohamed Babu would be a key political leader for Zanzibar and one of the charismatic great figures of revolutionary nationalism that had Comorian blood. As one of the Zanzibar migrant children, Abdulrahman Mohamed Babu was born in 1924, to a mother of Arabo and Oromo descent and a father of Comorian origin.

In London, Babu became aware of the need for internationalist solidarity after World War Two. He sought to make contacts around the region. In his home country of Comoros, he collaborated closely with peasant masses, especially with producers of cloves.

In Zanzibar, he joined the Zanzibar National Party (ZNP) and became secretary-general. Later, after choosing "the camp of Engels", he decided on founding the UMMA party for the "ideas of Marx, Lenin, Engels, and Mao Tse Tung" (Patriomine, 2008, para. 5).

As a key leader, Babu met Che Guevara, Malcolm X, Angela Davis, Fidel Castro, and was in contact with the People's Republic of China, Cuba, Palestine, Democratic People's Republic of Korea, and the German Democratic Republic.

Upon the creation and union of Tanganyika and Zanzibar, Babu became a minister of Julius Nyerere in charge of the economy. Trying to keep Nyerere committed to the ideals was difficult, and Nyerere would relieve him. Babu would continue the fight for the "camp of Engels" from Tanzania instead of Comoros. It is a wonder why a personality like Babu with so much influence as one of the key organizers amongst the Comorian diaspora in Zanzibar, and with great international connections even a part of Nyerere's close advisor, would not want to help with progression of Comoros socialism and independence. When his home country declared independence, he decided to not take part in Comoros's experiment in socialism. Babu would have been a major experienced organizer, even possibly contending Ali Soilihi for leadership.

Regardless of many Comorians like Babu taking part in Tanzanian and Zanzibar revolutions, these revolutions proved to be a rupturing phenomenon for exiled and political Comorians. Many were jailed, killed, and repatriated back to the archipelago for their apparent Arabness. Furthermore, the Zanzibar Revolution resulted in an upsurge of the Comorian ruling class. When Babu's UMMA participated, it was a watershed of possible racial violence of Comorians in the archipelago because of the closeness of Arab identity and to French authorities' connection to the ASP (Roberts, 2021). UMMA's participation in Comorian politics had implications for racial dynamics and the potential for violence within the archipelago. It underscores the complex interplay of ethnic, regional, and political factors in shaping the social and political landscape of Comoros during this period.

Specifically targeting MOLINACO as plotters of 'ideologies' and 'foreigners", Comorian reformist Saïd Mohamed Cheikh wanted to create division and attack MOLINACO's rights as an independence and nationalist movement organized by authentic Comorians.

On the contrary to MOLINACO's nationalist reformist and even centrist stands, leaders in Ngazidja formed the Socialist Party for the Liberation of Comoros (Parti socialiste pour la libération des Comores, or PSLC). These leaders, unlike the Zanzibari-Comorian MOLINACO, established connections on many islands.

The Comorian ruling class banned the PSLC and put its leaders in prison. Still as a French Quisling, Cheikh made a declaration that 'those who desire independence only aim to sow poverty, to reap power in disorder and revolution,' threatening to use 'machine guns' against them (Roberts, 2021).

When PSLC was destroyed, the ruling class of the archipelago made clear that any anti-colonialist nationalism would not happen in Comoros.

Despite the fact that the first Comorian diaspora was not created by political exile, the second exile was political when the Cheikh slammed any organization promoting independence from France. To unite the Comorian diaspora, MOLINACO, especially its women's section, called for unity from its Dar es Salaam headquarters. Nationalism of the MOLINACO variant gave space and resources while in this exile stage (Roberts, 2021).

Many Comorians did not want to join MOLINACO because of the possible chaos without having French imperialist protections and a French passport. The Comorian Association broke from MOLINACO because of the happenings of the Zanzibar Revolution.

MOLINACO was seen by a younger generation of conscious Comorians, who saw the group as a place to receive education abroad. MOLINACO obtained student scholarships to study in Eastern European socialist countries as well as the Soviet Union (Roberts, 2021).

MOLINACO's efforts to support education and provide opportunities for students from Comoros to study abroad, particularly in socialist countries, indicates a strategic approach to building human capital and fostering international solidarity among students aligned with the organization. For political support from liberation movements, MOLINACO received assistance from

FRELIMO. FRELIMO took MOLINACO documents and translated to English as well as the support of the OAU Liberation Committee.

The Comorian diaspora and archipelagic nature of Comorian independence were on the periphery of other nationalist movements and leaders. For instance, Julius Nyerere refused to bring up the issue with France.

Because of the reactionary positions that Comoros was not "African", trying to support MOLINACO had many troubles from Zanzibar and Tanzania activists. So much so that the youth wing of the ASP demanded the Comorians to 'go home' regarding Comorian's connection to feudalistic sultans as well as racism in Tanzania questioning Comorian Africanness (Walker, 2021).

The complex dynamics surrounding identity, power, and belonging within Comorian society and the broader African context. It suggests that these issues were subject to debate and contestation, particularly among youth and political organizations like the ASP.

MOLINACO in Madagascar

On the contrary to MOLINACO in Tanzania, a more possible positive outlook in Madagascar was the goal than the reality. This reality gives insight into the future riots and massacres against Comorians in Mahajanga years later.

Because Madagascar connection to French imperialism and not a socialist homeland like Tanzania (albeit ambivalent and hostile) of which to work from, Malagasy condemned, banned, expelled, and event went out to destroy MOLINACO.

The president of Madagascar, Philibert Tsiranana supported Said Mohammed Cheik's legitimacy of Comorian bourgeois-nationalism as well as supported South Africa's apartheid (Roberts, 2021). It suggests that Tsiranana's support for these ideologies and regimes may have influenced regional politics and relationships during the period in question.

Wanting to continuously work in Madagascar, MOLINACO made repeated attempts to implant itself there. The growing work of MOLINACO influence, if any, made many Malagasy want to control the destinies of both Madagascar and Comoros by creating the 'Social Democratic Party of Madagascar and Comoros.' This is regardless of whether any Comorians had any voice or membership to this party.

Tsiranna pushed his own legitimacy as a defender of the interest of Comoros without any regard for Comorian's self-determination nor recognizing MOLINACO. While in Moroni in 1965, Tsiranna claimed that 'the French are our number one friends and so our Comorian brothers from Comoros are therefore our friends twice over . . . .. "The Comorians constitute the nineteenth tribe of Madagascar where they live as genuine children of the island country (Roberts, 2021, p. 56)."

With all these developments, MOLINACO tried to make connections, push their literature, and stay connected with developments on the home archipelago, while dealing with internal strife that resulted from members being from different islands

Internal strife between MOLINACO political factions and islandic factions also disowned MOLINACO by making headway. The group was controlled mostly by Nzazidjian-Comorians, which made Ndzuanin-Comorians less interested in supporting.

Many Comorian nationalists and anti-colonialists in Mahajanga, Madagascar were members of the pro-Moscow Congress Party for the Independence of Madagascar. Because of the contention between Moscow and Beijing, MOLINACO collaborated with the Chinese-aligned group Madagascar for the Malagasy. Due to internal strife and infighting, these opposition movements created ambiguous fiefdoms over parts of Madagascar for each group (Roberts, 2021).

The Madagascar government turned OAU opinion against Comorian independence, aligning with other Third World solidarity movements—even after the OAU called for Comoros to be in the UN alongside other anti-colonialist countries. Madagascar continued its support for Saïd Mohamed Cheikh as the legitimate Comorian stakeholder, rather than MOLINACO.

Tsiranna explained to the Malagasy government that Comorian activists stationed in Madagascar should return to Comoros, as they were not speaking for the whole of the archipelago. As per Tsiranna, these Comorian activists "should go there and confer with their brothers, the real Comorians, and then discuss with France" (Roberts, 2021, p. 45).

Like the revolutionary change in Tanzania, which accelerated problems for MOLINACO, Madagascar experienced a revolution as well—one that would shift the political environment in which MOLINACO pursued its goals.

Despite a revolution happening in Madagascar forcing Tsiranna from power in 1972, and the new government breaking off with French and apartheid South Africa, a more favorable revolutionary-regime became closer geographically to Comoros. MOLINACO leaders could work under better circumstances.

MOLINACO requested legitimacy as a Comorian nationalist group from Madagascar in 1974 to work there officially. At the time of this demand, the deal was not needed.

MOLINACO, in its dealings with diasporan Comorian leaders, Tanzanian, and Madagascar divisiveness, spent its diminutive work organizing for the revolution on the archipelago and not for equality in Madagascar.

Regardless of all the work with OAU and trying to gain trust in African leaders and other groups, nothing seemed to gain root (Roberts, 2021). The years of work over a vast continent and trials of aggravating united front-style work did not mean it was granted political power and legitimacy on the archipelago.

When the archipelago independence struggle finally had momentum, it could not be stopped. One of the many student strikes and revolts in Comoros occurred in January 1968. Momentum for independence happened quickly when in 1970 Saïd Mohamed Cheikh died and his moderate course faltered. One group created on the archipelago after the student strikes was the *Socialist Party of Comoros (Parti socialiste des Comores*, or PASOCO) and entered work with MOLINACO. Regarding the Socialist Party, it was largely supported by students and other young people (Walker,2019). Before any work could be done, both groups split and in 1971. From this split, MOLINACO created the *Party for the Evolution of Comoros (parti pour l'Évolution des Comores)*.

Comorian ruling class supported MOLINACO and other diaspora and stated that '[w]e are Comorians of African origin, we are not short of friends 'If we take independence, we're not going to die of hunger (Roberts, p. 123, 2021)." When the independence struggle finally made on the archipelago, it resulted in personality-parties being created and trying to contend for power, without any of the fruits of the labor that MOLINACO desperately tried to grow.

Another group of Comorian exiles flourished for a time before independence. Like Ali Soilihi, emerging petty bourgeois and bourgeoise youth went to France or Galliéni high school in Antananarivo, Madagascar. They benefited from scholarship to learn how to manage the state and business as Comoros received autonomy from France. Many Comorians also went to Paris, Bordeaux, and Toulouse. They will be joined in 1966 by a second contingent formed in the very young high school of Moroni. In France, the students formed the Association of students and Trainees from the Comoros in France (AESC). The group was formed to create connections and cultural events.

During this formation, the archipelago was going through independence and conflict. To distance themselves from the student strikes in 1964, and from the MOLINACO, PASOCO, and PEC independence movements, AESC distanced themselves to be as apolitical as possible. To AESC, connecting to politics will mean stepping out of bounds by the French administration and deny funds for Francophone student groups in Africa. In 1968, however, the group took in favor of independence.

Gradually the AESC group purged its ambiguously pro-France line and took over a more radical "Democratic centralist" approach. They would organize in cells and have an Executive Committee based on Maoist China and socialist Albania models. Marxism-Leninism and the quotations of

Mao were the main theoretical tenants of the group. Literature with analysis of international events and Comorian events were increasingly needed to be dispensed to the crescendo of independence fever of Comoros. Revolutionary discipline through Marxist framework was part of the day-to-day structure. Ex-ASEC member Ibrahim Mohamed Sidi said that the organization taught him a lot about imperialism of France and the United States as well as the revolution in the Global South:

> "ASEC was a school. I was curious to learn things that I didn't know about my country. The political context, for example. When I came to the meetings of the CBs, people exposed themes on the Comoros that I discovered, when I came from there. I admit that I liked it so much that I went there spontaneously, especially since it was on campus (Saindou, 2022, para 15)."

The importance of education and curiosity in deepening one's understanding of political issues and national identity of Comoros afar. It also underscores the role of community engagement and discussion forums, such as meetings of the CBs, in fostering learning and dialogue about important themes related to the Comoros.

As liberatory consciousness grew, positions were taken that the group would be anti-revisionist, pro-China, and pro-Albania. Executive Committee leaders made a trip both to visit with Mao and Hoxha. The zeal that this tiny group of such a tiny country only springs the imagination what they wanted to accomplish in the belly of the beast for a future socialist Comoros is outstanding (Sainou,2022). Relations with the French comrades predominantly included the Communist Party of France M-L (PCMLF), and Union of Revolutionary Communist Youth. International contacts included with other student groups in Vietnam, Cambodia, Peru, Chile, Spain, and Madagascar as well other liberation struggles (Saindou,2022).

Cameroonian Maoist economist Ahmed Ouled writes how the ASEC is part of the independence of Comoros yet, claims that the Soilihist revolution was a counterrevolution. Ouled's writing is the only proof that there was such a bureaucracy that took over the Comorian revolution. Ouled's thesis is that there was a healthier variant of the revolution and then as per Ouled, Soilihi was a counterrevolutionary to a much more unfettered Comorian democracy and socialism. Yet there was no bureaucratic caste in Solihist Comoros. But Ouled believes that:

> "From this aura, ASEC will play an influential role in the struggle for the independence of the Comoros. She is alongside PASOCO in the United Patriotic Front, before denouncing the alliance of this party with the United National Front around Ali Soilih. It denounces Ali Soilih's "pseudo-revolution" and suspects the National Revolutionary Council (CNR), which emerged from the coup d'etat which brought Ali Soilih to power of attempting to "recruit youth" and "liquidate the patriotic movement   (Saindou, 2022, para 30).

ASEC expressed suspicions regarding the National Revolutionary Council (CNR), which emerged from the coup d'état that brought Ali Soilih to power. ASEC accused the CNR of attempting to recruit youth and of seeking to "liquidate" the patriotic movement, suggesting concerns about the CNR's intentions and tactics. If Ouled's prognosis is valid, then who or what groupings were the vanguard party? And if so, should we quarrel and squabble over Comorians first emergence breaking fetters of many oppressing and reactionary "isms" that in its only history thus far was 3 years of socialist democracy. The revolution was born with Soilihi's coup.

Greens, Whites, and Reds on the Archipelago

Slowly but surely impacted by the revolutionary anti-colonialist movements in Africa, a growing number of politically conscious Comorians, resenting the French neglect of the Comoros Islands, supported independence on the archipelago. Independence-minded Comorians, especially younger ones, were energized by dramatic events across the Mozambique Channel and on the African mainland.

But politics on the archipelago in the 1960s were dominated by a social and economic elite, largely descendants of the precolonial sultanate ruling families, which was conservative and pro-French.

During Comoros' period of self-government as an overseas department, there were two main conservative political groupings: the Parti Vert (Green Party), which later became known as the Comoros Democratic Union (Union Démocratique des Comores, UDC), and the Parti Blanc (White Party), later reconstituted as the Democratic Assembly of the Comoran People (Rassemblement Démocratique du Peuple Comorien, RDPC).

Dr. Said Mohamed Cheikh, president of the Parti Vert and of the Governing Council, was, until his death in 1970, the most important political leader in the islands.

The Parti Blanc, under Prince Said Ibrahim, provided the opposition, endorsing a progressive program that included land reform and loosening of the monopoly on Comorian cash crops enjoyed by the foreign-owned plantation sociétés.

In 1946, Said Ibrahim was appointed Governor, and later became a member of the National Assembly. He then served as Minister of Finance from 1957 to 1958. In 1959, Comoros gained two seats in the French National Assembly, while still remaining a single electoral district. From 1958 to 1970, Ibrahim was elected and continuously re-elected as president of the Territorial Assembly and the Chamber of Deputies of the Comoros.

Despite growing calls from the national bourgeoisie for independence, Said Ibrahim advocated only for cooperation between France and Comoros, as if both nations were on equal footing.

The second most powerful member of the Parti Vert, Ahmed Abdallah, was a wealthy plantation owner of the company Addullah et Filis and a representative to the French National Assembly. He succeeded Cheikh as president of the Governing Council soon after Cheikh died.

In 1972, Abdallah, now leader of his political party, the Comoros Democratic Union (UDC), became president of the government council and Chief Minister of the Comoros. He served in that position until 6 July 1975, when the islands became independent from France—apart from Maore/Mayotte, which voted to remain part of France.

Abdallah became the first president of the independent islands and was later overthrown in the coup that provided space for Soilhi to create socialism (Walker, 2019).

Well into the 1960s, the two established parties were concerned primarily with maintaining a harmonious relationship with France while obtaining assistance in economic planning and infrastructure development. Given this consensus, politically active Comorians often based their allegiance on personal feelings toward Ahmed Abdallah or Ibraim, who led the two main parties, and on whatever patronage either party could provide.

Abdallah, although a conservative bourgeois politician, saw independence as a "regrettable necessity," given the unsatisfactory level of French support and the growing alienation of an increasingly radicalized younger generation. The violent suppression of a student demonstration in 1968 and the death of Said Mohammed Cheikh in 1970 provided further evidence of the erosion of the existing Francophonic order in Comoros.

In 1972, leaders of the Parti Vert (now the UDC) and the Parti Blanc (now the RDPC) agreed to press for independence, hoping at the same time to maintain cordial relations with France. A coalition of conservative and moderate parties, the Party for the Evolution of Comoros (Parti pour l'Évolution des Comores), was at the forefront of the independence effort. The coalition excluded PASOCO, which it perceived as violently revolutionary, but it cooperated for a time with MOLINACO.

During 1973 and 1974, the local government negotiated with France and issued a "Common Declaration" on June 15, 1973, defining how the islands would gain independence. Part of the backdrop of the negotiations was a pro-independence riot in November 1973 in Moroni, during which the buildings of the Chamber of Deputies were burned.

A referendum was held on December 22, 1974. Voters supported independence by a 95 percent majority, but 65 percent of those casting ballots on Mahore/Mayotte chose to remain as a French department.

The next stage would define Comoros in its own way, on its own ground. To make socialism in Comoros a reality, a Mongozi would be needed to help turn the small archipelago into a unique experience—an experiment in archipelagic revolution.

Enter The Mongozi: Ali Soilihi

"I said that we want to carry out a lucid revolution" Ali Soilihi on March 31, 1976. - (Damir Ben Ali,2009)."

Ali Soilihi's collected works and notes would not survive the revolution. Unlike many revolutionary leaders, writing any biography or continuity regarding his life, theory, and praxis is difficult during the day-to-day revolution. Like Lenin, sometimes one is too busy with the revolution to write about it.

The future Mongozi (meaning "Guide" in Swahili) Ali Soilihi was born on January 7, 1937, in Majunga, Madagascar. His mother was from the city of Chouani, and his father was from the city of Ntsoudjini. At the age of twenty-one, he passed an entrance exam to the agricultural high school in Ambatobé, Madagascar, later mastering the French language. Eventually he had another training period at an agro-technical school near Paris. In Paris it is rumored that he took part in the 1968 revolution and contacted the French Communist Party, although they did not agree with their pro-Moscow line (Bellatou, interview 2022). Soilihi may have navigated various ideological currents and organizational ties while participating in the political ferment of the time.

Once he graduated, Soilihi returned to the Comoros and worked in agriculture for two years. Afterwards, he obtained an internship in France to the Agricultural Production Development Office (BDPA). After an internship in the Tropical Agriculture Teaching Establishment of Nogent, he followed an internship at the Institute for the

Study of Economic and Social Development. Returned to the Comoros, he was appointed Director of the Comoros Economic Development Company (SODEC) (Comores-online.com). His appointment to a key position within the economic sphere of the Comoros upon their return to the country created efforts to drive economic growth and development in the nation.

In 1964 Soilihi was made President of the Economic Development Society of the Comoros then elected to the Territorial Assembly in 1968 and served as Minister of Public Works in 1970 to 1972. In August 1967, he was elected deputy and later Said Ibrahim appointed him Minister of Equipment and Tourism in September 1970.

His activism would take priority then being reticent over the emerging Comorian bureaucracy. Dini Nassur discussed a strike that Soilihi took a forefront of leadership in:

> "hundreds of them left to try to stop the strike but Soilihi and his militants diverted them from their goal. Then when the army arrested about twenty of us, it was Ali Soilihi who taught us how to make Molotov cocktails in his field! And during our hunger strike, he was, along with Doctor Tourqui, the only political leader we accepted among us. He brought us water but did not give us lessons like the others. What turned out to be later policy and creation of the Moissy, when later he

> appealed to the youth, and we said we had to help him (Giachino, 2005a, para 12)."

Taking part in some strikes, Soilihi became a rising star within the Comoros independent movement but not becoming a member to any of the established parties such as Verti, Blanc, and MOLINACO. Sollihist activist Aboudou writes on how to Soilihist revolution was still an incipient idea for Soilihi and Comoros.

> "In 1975, the idea of revolution was far from ripe for Soilihi. It imposed itself as a political necessity under the pressure of the difficult circumstances that it had to face or disappear (Kweli,2018)." Despite this initial reluctance, Soilihi was compelled to embrace the idea of revolution due to external pressures and difficult circumstances facing his administration. These circumstances may have included internal unrest, external threats, or socio-economic challenges that necessitated radical action. But planning occurred with many Comorian politicians visiting Paris met with students, intellectuals and other Comorians living in Paris, at the Grand Hotel, to discuss the state of their country. "For a Comorian sailor Aboudou Mohamed Youssouf the life-changing encounter takes place in Paris, with Soilihi. It was during one of these meetings that he was noticed by a Comorian politician named Ali Soilihi (Gitachino, 2005b, para 6)".

The transformative nature of encounters with influential individuals and the potential for such interactions to shape the course of one's life. It also underscores the significance of connections made in diverse settings, such as

Paris, in the context of Comorian individuals' experiences and aspirations.

Aboudou Mohamed Youssouf grapples with the implications of Ali Soilihi's request and the potential consequences of political involvement in his role as a sailor. It reflects the complexities and dilemmas faced by individuals when navigating the intersection of personal convictions and professional responsibilities. Aboudou Mohamed Youssouf continues "his (author's note: Soilihi) request intrigued me greatly, but who was he really? What did he want from me? Moreover, as a sailor, we did not have to get involved in politics and I was afraid that people would tell my superiors that I was involved in politics (Kweli,2018, para 7)."

Yet the future guide of the Comorian Revolution, convinces Aboudou to return to the Comoros with simple words:

"the country will need people like you." Aboudou does not know then that the future Mongozi Soilhi is recruiting him for the revolution.

In 1972 Ali Soilihi became Minister of Equipment, entrusting Aboubou unofficially with missions in the country. In his unofficial role, Aboudou says "he asked me to go and supervise, or rather to monitor the work that the road workers were doing [...] He sent me to pick up equipment and bring it back to different places to help the farmers of his movement (Kweil, 2018, para 7)."

Soon time would show that Soilihi's recruit would be needed for revolution. Action and progression were snowballing for the Comoros.

Following a 1974 referendum that indicated almost unanimous popular support for independence on the three westernmost islands but reticence in Maore/Mayotte, Ahmed Abdallah, President of the territorial assembly, unilaterally declared independence in July 1975.In November of 1975, Comoros became the 143rd member of the UN, defined as all four islands, but the vote kept Maore/Mayotte under French control.

Furthermore, irked by Comorian temerity, France withdrew all economic and technical support for the young state, thus encouraging the establishment of a radical revolutionary regime under Ali Soilihi.A movie clip by the Fondation Mtsahiya, documents that the revolution "cannot be run in a traditional and feudal way (Fondation Mtsahiya, 2018)."

Ali Soilih's decision to pursue revolution was driven by a commitment to addressing class-based inequalities and challenging the oppressive structures of imperialism, aligning him with the revolutionary ideals espoused by figures like Che Guevara and Fidel Castro.

Time to liberate Maore?

During socialism in Comoros, there was the anecdote of when a phone call from an organizer would get a phone call from another organizer they would ask "You ready to liberate Maore?" If the answer is in the affirmative then the call would continue (Kweli,2024).

The fourth island Maore/Mayotte would be continually contested during initial independence movements and contemporary attacks against neo-colonialism. Maore/Mayotte's land area is 374 square kilometers (144 sq mi) about the size of Ramsey County, Minnesota. There is a modern misconception that the basis of reasons why of its uneven social-economic and political development with the rest of the archipelago is that unlike the other islands predominantly Muslim and Maore is predominantly Christian (Kweli,2024). This is false since all the islands were settled by Islamic traders and settlers.

Comoros pressed its claim under "Question of the Comorian Island of Mayotte" to the UN General Assembly, OAU, Non-Aligned Countries Movement, and Organization of Islamic Cooperation. Mayotte formed no part of the state that France finally recognized in December of 1975.

From the MOLINACO position, and from Marxist self-determination, Comorian liberation does not end with only three of the four major islands. In the Latimer Ranger interview, Soilihi is quite clear that the Comoros islands in French law dictated that Comorian islands are all four islands. Soilihi insists that "this always involved the territory of the Comoro Islands consisting of four islands. French legislation is quite formal on that. (Ranger, 1976, p 6)."

Due to de Gaullism in France trying to save face from the breaking of its overseas empire most notably Vietnam and Algeria, this fragmented policy of Comoros territory was due to French working. No matter how one sees how weak Comorian nationalism or groups supporting or working towards Comorian nationalism are, Comoros includes all islands on the archipelago.

Contrary to the other islands wanting full independence, Maore political groupings wanted a firm tether to France. The Mouvement Populaire Mahorais (MPM), lobbied for territory status to create public need to vote against independence (Walker, 2019).

When the left-nationalist Comorian bourgeoisie led by Ahmend Abdallah wanted a unanimous break from France, Maore voted to be a French department. De Gaullist France supported and honored the referendum held island by island instead of the whole archipelago as a single vote regarding independence.

In the most radicalized spirit of African anti-colonialism, it is absurd that a people would vote to be continually tethered to a Western imperialist state (Roberts, 2021).

This strong stance against colonialism and imperialism, advocating for the full emancipation of African nations and the rejection of any form of continued subordination to the Western powers. It underscores the importance of independence, self-determination, and liberation in the pursuit of African sovereignty.

The Maorais People's Movement worked denouncing independence and maintained vigorously Maore stay an overseas territory.

MOLINACO wanted to work with MPM, since both were on the surface anti-colonial, MPM disregarded any work with organizations who worked towards independent, possibly socialist, nationalist Comoros.

Amamaye Idriss (2006) supports the conclusion that MOLINACO worked tirelessly within tightly controlled places such as Tanzania and Madagascar against colonialism and imperialism at all costs. Whereas the MPM was more reformist and open working with French colonialist means.

As per Amamaye Idriss writes in Roberts (2022), MPM proved more "successful" than MOLINCO of gaining freedoms for itself than uniting with the rest of archipelago.

MPM was for self-determination of Marois to decide its destiny, but one can argue that Maore-Comorians did not see themselves as a distinct nation or nationalism with/or Comoros, but a part of the common Francophone identity.

France wanted its own hold of Comoros, after the rest of the archipelago decided on unilateral independence. Many times, in history, imperialists have deployed Marxist jargon to defend bourgeois interest and "solidarity" and the right of self-determination in militaristic defenses of Kuwait, Republic of Korea (South Korea), and Israel.

Revolutionaries and anti-imperialists of all stripes must continue to advocate against French neo-colonialism of Maore and the union of Maoris with Comoros as part of Comorian destiny.

Against the self-determination of peoples, the Ministry of French Overseas Territories announced on October 1 that Paris would organize a separate referendum on Maroe.

Later, after the Comorian revolution was overturned, Sankara in his famous speech at the UN General Assembly remarked that "I do not wish to dwell too long on the question of Mayotte and the islands of the Malagasy archipelago; since the facts are clear and the principles obvious, there is no need to dwell on them. Mayotte belongs to the Comoros… (Sankara, 1984)."

Sankara's support for Comorian sovereignty over Mayotte and his willingness to address the issue on the global stage, emphasizing the clarity of the facts and principles underlying the dispute.

Abdallah Regime and Independence

When independence did come, Ahmend Abdallah, became the first president of Comoros. Abdallah's spearheaded the unilateral declaration of independence from France as well as, verbally attacking France over continued control over Maore, and thereby antagonizing the French government.

> "When the Comoros unilaterally declared independence from France in July 1975,7 the political scene was dominated by five small political parties, none of which had any clearly defined independence program of action above the level of simple sloganeering and the ritual condemnation of colonial rule, and none of which had a clearly defined national mass base. The largest political party, Oudzima, led by the first post-independence president, Ahmed Abdallah, held the majority in the colonial Chamber of Deputies, but it seemed to represent mainly the Island of Anjouan, Abdallah's home base. Three other parties (UMMA, the Comoro People's Democratic Rally, and the Comoro National Liberation Movement) were grouped together in the United National Front of the Comoros, an umbrella organization whose common political denominator was opposition to Abdallah's leadership. The fifth party, the Socialist Objective Party, functioned only intermittently (Mukonoweshuro,1990, p. 557)."

This fragmented and politically divided landscape in the Comoros at the time of independence declaration, with small parties lacking clear national agendas and opposition to Abdallah's leadership being a unifying factor for some factions. Internal intrigues among the Comorian elite provided a convenient entry point for external intervention, becoming the pattern of regime changes in the Comoros.

While the United National Front provided a legitimate alternative to the Abdallah regime, the UNF had no means to topple it. Specifically, the worried market of ylang-ylang for Chanel No. 5 counted on the endless supply of Comoros ylang-ylang for French markets.

Coup d' Ali Soilihi

Tensions later occurred between Abdullah and the French leading to the United National Front agitating to topple Ahmed Abdallah as a weak leader.

Particularly active was Yves Lebre, a well-connected Frenchman who had high level government contacts in Paris. Lebre was also well connected to the United National Front.

The owner of Air Comoros, immediately after the coup, he was appointed Comorian co-director in the Ministry of Foreign Affairs and subsequently roving ambassador to Europe.

It is possible that Lebre was a de facto broker between enemies of the Ahmend Abdallah regime and the mercenary-pirate Bob Denard.

As per Denard, meetings took place between contacts of De Gaulle, Gaullist capitalist Ferdinand Serre, Sultan Chauffoour representing Ali Soilhi. Yves Lebre, the director of Air-Comroes brokered the meeting regarding action against Abdullah. This coup "represents a great opportunity for the Comoros and France's interest in the Indian Ocean (Denard para 9)."

This imperialist opportunity was only a way of continued oppression by France, particularly in the context of France's strategic interests in the Indian Ocean region.

The August 3, 1975, coup was supported militarily by the French-born Bob Denard (an alias for Gilbert Bourgeaud, also known as Said Mustapha M'Hadjou) a veteran of wars of counterrevolution, and separatism from many countries to Indochina to Biafra. Many books written about him portray him as a swashbuckling hero-soldier. He is a product of French imperialism to contain and usurp the many revolutionary nationalist movements rupturing the Francophone empire.

On August 10th, the National Executive Council was created under control of Prince Said Mohammed Jaffar, and Soilihi was made Minister of Defense and Justice.

The revolution was tentatively under the real control of Soilihi and his mapidunzis (young militants, precursor to the Moissy).

In a discussion with Le Bret, Denard was told that he "will help Ali Soilih to take power by investing Anjouan to neutralize President Abdallah. When things are more clearly defined, you will train and mentor the militiamen with whom he will maintain order (Denard, para 10)."

Granted, Soilihi would be the main benefactor of the coup against the bourgeoisie led by Ahmed Abdallah, but directly the person who replaced him and was supported by the United National Front and the left-nationalist Said Mohamed Jaffar.

Did France not understand Soilihi's Marxist background, or did they feel that Soilihi would kowtow to French neo-colonialist control?

It seems later, that Soilihi was using Denard as a metaphorical train that Lenin used from Lake Geneva to the Finland Station.

Denard explains that the coup was launched on August 3:

> "While President Abdullah was visiting his village of Iconi on the island of Anjouan every Sunday. Ali Soilih launched an assault on his presidential residence and the radio building. He carried off his objective with only a few faithful armed with pistols and shotguns provided by Le Bret. After the rebellion spread through the city, Ali Soilih announced on the radio that he was establishing a curfew from 8p.m and handing over the fate of the country to a National Revolutionary Council (para 10)."

This indicates a move to consolidate power and establish a new governing body in the wake of the rebellion. This is a significant event in which Ali Soilihi seized control of key institutions and announced the establishment of a new governing council, signaling a shift in power dynamics within the country.

However, in a last stand, Abdullah had attempted to hive off his home base, Ndzuani /Anjouan, into a separate state. A determined military onslaught against Ndzuani/Anjouan, OAU mediation, and the subsequent arrest of Abdallah and his bodyguards neutralized these secessionist tendencies.

Habariza Comrores gives a more specific account regarding the political parties and the ambivalence of the coup on the Comorian masses:

> "On August 3, 1975, around 1:00 p.m....the airwaves of Radio Comoros announce the dismissal of the conservative regime carried by President Ahmed Abdallah and his notables from Udzima. Twenty-eight days after the declaration of independence, on August 3, 1975, a coalition of six political parties known as the United National Front overthrew the Abdallah government, with the aid of foreign mercenaries. Some observers claimed that French commercial interests, and possibly even the French government, had helped provide the funds and the matériel to bring off the coup. The reasons for the coup remain obscure, although the belief that France might return Mahoré if Abdallah were out of power appears to have been a contributing factor. Abdallah fled to Nzwani, his political power base, where he remained in control with an armed contingent of forty-five men until forces from Moroni recaptured the island and arrested him in late September 1975 (www.habariazacomores.com (2020), para, 14)."

The overthrow of President Abdallah's regime and the subsequent flight and arrest of Abdallah himself, raises questions about the complex dynamics surrounding French interests in the region. Furthermore, the knowledge of Soilihi's politics and Comorian politics at the advent of the coup was ambiguous to Denard, but not to Soilihi himself: meaning the:

> "work of elucidation of the conflicting, confused situation which goes from 72 to 75, not having been operated, the flash, dramatic passage of Ali Soilih in power has become only a myth which haunts the spirits, a political star that the little people listen all day long, waiting for a messiah who will never meet their hopes. We must therefore try to illuminate for us here and now, the incredible telescoping of three major events in this month of June - July 75: a unilateral declaration of independence, a coup d'état, the secession of the island of Mayotte...and ten years of unchallenged mercenary domination. It's a lot, it's even too much, for a small people stuck in a small archipelago, far from everything. This may explain the political sluggishness of the past thirty years. The Comorians have ultimately become a stunned, haggard, dispossessed people, unable to stop their descent into hell by themselves. It would be necessary to take each of these events and to explain it in itself but the dimensions of this article do not

allow it. The years between 72-75, constitutes a knot, a major point of articulation. All subsequent evolution of the Comoros with its violence, its upheavals, its disappointed hopes, and its serious injustices find here their soil which must be dug, if one wants to understand these thirty years of carnivalesque history. We have taken, notwithstanding the theoretical and political decision to focus attention on the August 3rd coup d'état and above all and above all to break with the commemorative apology of the great revolutionary or the anathema which excommunicates him by devoting him to the groans. We choose for our part, in all modesty, an analytical and critical approach that preserves both honesty and truth.

The origins of a large feudal family, the intellectual formation as well as the political and militant activity of Ali Soilih are very well-known facts in the country. But what are the reasons that led such intelligent and patriotic people to do the trick of August 3? Were they aware that by doing so they were compromising the audacity of independence and were going to engage the Comoros in an endless spiral? It is astonishing that a man as intelligent and honest as Ali Soilih did not want to explain the deep motives of his act (www.habariazacomores.com,2020,para15)"

This acknowledges that this period has become mythologized, with Soilihi's brief tenure in power symbolizing a political star that continues to captivate the imaginations of the people. The coup was possibly a revenge power grab for Soilihi against Prince Ibrahim and Jaffar. This drama goes back to how early politics in Comoros were based on personality loyalty then political lines.

Regarding the national assembly and the break occurring between Jaffar and Soilhi means that:

> "...in 1975 the deputies of the national assembly took the unprecedented historic decision to break with colonization by a unilateral declaration of independence, Ali Soilih then deputy as well as princes Said Ibrahim and Prince Said Mohamed Jaffar were absent from the Comoros. No one will know the nature of the discussions they had, the personalities they met and their influence. One can imagine the anger, the frustration if not the disappointment felt that such important political actors were somehow mystified, double-crossed and that they were sidelined from the biggest meeting in the history of the Comoros. My idea is therefore that the coup of August 3 is revenge for Ali Soilih to dismiss Abdallah and put his godfather in the saddle, the charismatic Prince and under his umbrella

> bide his time. Pure tactical and Machiavellian calculation. The question of the choice of the regime and particularly of the revolutionary option was not the explicit political project of August 3. Revolution will be an afterthought. The question of the revolution, its theoretical content, its conditions of realization, its personnel will be clarified progressively, piecemeal, and according to the circumstances. (www.habariazacomores.com (2020), para 16)."

The revolutionary agenda would emerge as an afterthought, with its theoretical content and personnel being clarified gradually over time, depending on the circumstances. This provides an interpretation of the coup of August 3, 1975, as a complex and strategic maneuver driven by personal ambitions, revenge, and a desire for political power, rather than an immediate commitment to revolutionary ideals. It suggests that the revolutionary agenda would evolve and become clearer in the aftermath of the coup.

In 1975, the Comoros won their independence, but it was an ambivalent independence, the anti-colonialist struggle was far from over. Comorians knew there would be much greater opportunities for liberation struggles and to create fathomable destiny: The sense of uncertainty and possibility that accompanied the announcement of the dismissal of President Ahmed Abdallah's regime on August 3, 1975, underscores the transformative nature of this political moment and its potential to reshape the trajectory of the Comoros.

During the coup, Ali Soilihi involves Aboudou, the reluctant sailor-activist, more in his process of conquest of power, by assigning him more "risky" missions. Soilihi chooses Aboudou to be his driver on August 3, 1975. Aboudou told that Soilihi tells him to fill the car with gas in the afternoon. When Soilihi got into the car, they headed towards the National Radio (www.habariazacomores.com, 2020, para 16).

In the early days of the revolution, the Mongozi Ali Soilihi made Aboudou Mohamed Youssouf responsible for a ministry with other comrades. The former sailor becomes a trusted man for the one who will be elected president of the new independent state.

From the events of September 5, 1975, Denard later discusses the details of the plan. Placed on the tarmac of the Moroni airport, under the auspices of French gendarmes, Denard unloads some three hundred rifles to support and train the new revolutionary Comorian army:

> "Ali Soilihi receives me and explains to me, with a precision that betrays his intelligence, what he expects of me. This man, who is not forty years old, is far from being unanimous among the French and workers who remained in Moroni. Not only does he not hide it from them, but I verify that it only a few hours after our meeting. As I cross Iconi, a European rush at me with his car, which I narrowly avoid. Hayaya airport officials then tried to put a spoke in our wheels. As I come to receive a last delivery of equipment. They threaten

> to prevent the landing of Mallock's plane if I do not move away from the edge of the runway (Denard, year unknown, para 28)."

Denard quickly realizes the truth of Soilihi's statements when faced with hostile actions from the French rushing at them with a car and airport officials attempting to hinder their activities. These incidents highlight the tensions and challenges surrounding Soilihi's leadership and Denard's involvement in their shared endeavors.

Near Itsoudzou camp in the north of Grande Comoros, Denard trained for two days with two hundred Comorians of Soilihi mapinduzi (militants).

Denard complains with racist arrogance on how Comorians are "allergic to the smell of gunpowder and detonations. Carefully, I entrust them with rifles without ammunition (Denard, para 29)."

Denard is aware of mapinduzi anxiety but still finds a way to contribute to the situation, ensuring safety by providing weapons without the potential for use. This demonstrates a Eurocentric approach to managing their condition while still participating in activities that require them to handle radicalized Comorians with firearms.

Yet, to send combatants without ammunition shows the perplexity having a racist mercenary train the amateur yet affirming freedom fighters.

This structure gives space to the contradictions and critiques embedded in the narrative. Let me know if you'd like help formatting the quote or building transitions into the next section.

Continuing to use Denard for the Revolution, Soilihi orders Denard to scour the island for Abdullahist opponents and to parade the mapinduzi in a show of force. In Denard's writings:

> "{t}he Minister of Defense, who is keen to assert his power, asks me to organize a parade of his troops in Moroni without uniforms. I therefore push for the 'one, two,' and, convinced that they will create an illusion by their mere cohesion, cap my recruits with a pink and white scarf. After having split them into two companies of four sections, I lead them to Moroni. When my two companies pass, shouting a chat of paratroopers, Infront of the Poste De Moroni, still guarded by French soldiers. The population cannot guess that these soldiers have still not touched ammunition. As for Ali Soilih, who is not a soldier but an agricultural engineer, he is content with the false impression of strength that emerges from my children's sections (Denard para 14)."

Denard's role in organizing a parade of troops in Moroni at the request of the Minister of Defense at the time, Ali Soilihi, happened with troops not having uniforms, as well as leading them in a march, using coordinated movements to create the illusion of cohesion. To enhance this illusion, the speaker caps the recruits with pink and white scarves. Dividing them into two companies with four sections each, the speaker leads them through Moroni, where they pass in front of the Poste De Moroni, still guarded by French soldiers.

The population is unaware that the troops are unarmed, and Ali Soilihi, content with the false impression of strength conveyed by the parade, observes the spectacle. This promotion, like the burning of the archives later, shows that Soilihi has a knack to create the illusion of strength.

One such account of demonstration of force against Abdullahism in a village a couple of grenades are flung by a Cessana by Air Comoros. Denard, who has been the epitome of the counter revolutionary pirate all over Africa, supports the Marxist Soilihi.

Denard writes "I address the villager a speech extolling the merits of the democracy which is being set up in Moroni under the aegis of Ali Soilhi (para 15)." Other fly-bys from Air Comoros present demonstrations against Abdullah with shooting against tarmacs and landing beaches.

Denard discusses the fait accompli that is given to the opposition of the greater firepower that Denard/Soilihi have. Denard writes that "Abdallah was alerted from the first detonations. He quickly puts on women's clothes, flees from his villa in Ouani and takes refuge in his stronghold of Domoni. After a short pounding with mortars, I only discovered, in his residence, a few guns and a large stock of rice which I distribute to the population (para 7)."

Continued opposition by Abdullahist opponents by fifty or some men. They are quickly dispersed or disappeared by Denard gunfire. One man refusing to be captured but as Denard in his memoirs writes that he is faking madness to stop being shot

After the coup, a three-man directorate took control. One of the three, Ali Soilihi, was appointed Minister of Defense and Justice and subsequently was made head of state by the Chamber of Deputies on January 3, 1976. Four days earlier, on December 31, 1975, France had formally recognized the independence of Comoros (minus Mahoré). The Umma radio station declared "[i]n the name of the people, today is a great day. The government of Ahmend Abdallah is no more (Weinberg,1994p.35)." Abdallah is later given a diplomatic passport and sent to Libya.

Soilihi at the time was the real power while having Prince Said Mohamed Jaffar as temporary head of state. The Jaffar regime was characterized by general paralysis and lack of concrete action. This is because it was concerned more with spoil-sharing than with rational administration.

The now ruling National Revolutionary Council was composed of six parties with conflicting interests and each ministry had two ministers pursuing a variety of contradictory personal interests. Such an arrangement was hardly conducive to efficient government.

Populist measures such as the regime's decision to expel all French authorities and Denard's mercenaries were met with hostility and suspicion, after months of continuing animosity between Denard and Soilihi. There is no evidence that Denard felt tricked by Soilihi's hints of anti-French policies. Denard later in his reminisces made the link between Denard and Soilihi.

There is no evidence that Denard felt tricked by Soilihi's hints of anti-French policies. Denard later in his reminisces made the link between the mapinduzi and the Moissy.

There is also a great discovery in the following passage of Soilihi being an advocate and supporter of socialism with Comorian characteristics, if not its brainchild. This first evidence of discovery of 'Comorian-style Marxism', and it takes Denard to mention it, even if it's a nonchalant mention. Denard discusses Soilihi with his countenance being:

> "face puffy and his gaze so expressionless. The man who looks down on me no longer has anything to do with the man who, a few months ago, counted on my protection and my advice. A supporter of Comorian-style Marxism, he boasts of having dismantled a conspiracy hatched in Moroni by a dozen of his opponents. He no longer trusts anyone but his female bodyguards, the best militiamen I trained, and above all the old Mapinduzis with whom he formed the Moissi commando in memory of the first man who fell during the conquest of Anjouan. I abandoned Ali Soilihi without regret to his Marxist dreams (para 78)."

Denard observes that Soilihi, who once relied on their protection and advice, now seems distant and disconnected. To Denard, Soilihi has become distrustful of others, relying only on his bodyguards and militiamen trained by the Denard and old Mapinduzis.

Whether Soilihi was planning to remove Jaffar to pursue a socialist agenda or wait Jaffar out is not known. The abject poverty afflicting most Comorians did not appear a subject of government concern under Prince Said Mohamed Jaffar.Some islands of the archipelago, in the beginning stages of forming an independent capitalist state, experienced growing famine and unemployment (Walker, 2018). Subsidized French-imported rice, reaching up to 15,000 tons per year, was automatically stopped by France. These policies did not validate the Jaffar leadership to create self-sufficient food organization in Comoros.

The situation was used to pivot from French subsidies to World Food Program aid. Jaffar established a rice company that was owned 51 percent by the Swiss (Walker, 2018). This was a trick to fool the masses, since the state had no purchasing power. The government remained largely on paper. Basic goods were to be wanted by the masses. By January 1976, the state had only enough money to pay civil servants.This connection to capitalism was one of the main intent variables left over by the French ancien régime and was later abolished in Soilihist socialism.

Ahmed Abdallah and Prince Said Mohamed Jaffar did not hold office long enough to pursue any sort of agenda or establish any progressive state. Jaffar gave power to Ali Soilihi and Soilihi moved hastily to cement himself in the presidential palace of Beit-Salam. What happened to Comoros would shape Comoros in an unforeseen way. Parti Blanc rival Saïd Ibrahim Ben Ali would later pass away and lead to Soilhi's rise to destiny. Comorian writer "Ankili" says that:

> "Unexpected death of Prince Said Ibrahim on (Author's note: December 20, 1975) 1975 will sound like a thunderclap. This death will upset Ali Soilihi's organization chart, his agenda, the pace of implementation of his projects. It will have deprived him of a capital support which he would need for a certain time to face the resistance of the Comorians and particularly the customary feudal systems (https://countrystudies.us/comoros/4.htm)"

In the time between independence, the coup, and Prince Said Ibrahim's death, Soilihi was forced to bring about rapid change.

Soilihi was given an opportunity to create a Comorian-style socialist society. Ali Soilihi managed to mark a turning point in contemporary history. The revolutionary experience from January 1976 to May 1978 constituted the first time a liberated and free Comoros was not fettered by France and world imperialism.

Pink March to Liberate Maore!

At the time of the Soilihi coup, the continued liberation of Maore was on the agenda. During the Ranger interview, of which Ranger and French Radio International asked the new president Ali Soilihi of Comoros, regarding the

Moissy, Mayotte, and as well as internal affairs. Involving Mayotte, Soilihi hid no allusion that Mayotte was Comorian. Soilihi told Ranger that "[m]y attitude toward Mayotte is the attitude of the entire Comorian people The Comoro Islands are the Comoro Islands. (Ranger, 1976, p.7)." Later, as the socialist constitution later stated with words from Ali Soilihi himself:

> "The permanent struggle for the reintegration of the Comorian island Mayotte. In the concerts of the Nations, France had several times used its right of veto at the UN. And to date, no country in the world has recognized the legitimacy of France on the Comorian island of Mayotte, to my knowledge. A country smaller than the city of Marseilles knew how to sensitize the world including the unconditional allies of France in the concerts of the Nations. (Nouvelle Soilihste Generation,2020)."

As per Denard, right after the coup, Maore/Mayotte was next on the list to include all of Comoros. Denard would help Soilihi take power in Comoros, but Comoros, to Denard did not include Mayotte. As per Denard this is the conversation between him and Soilihi before the Pink March debacle:

> "Soilihi: If the King of Morocco organized a green march to ensure his sovereignty over the Spanish Sahara a few days ago. I

am going to launch a pink march on Mayotte. I want you to prepare for this operation.

Denard: Mr. President, it is not foreseen in our agreements that I go against my country's interests in any way. I will therefore not follow you in this manner (Denard, para 34)."

They argued and Soilihi told Denard to confine himself to Comorian army interests. Denard discusses the operation of the so-called Pink March that took place after the August 1975 coup that put Soilihi in power:

"At dawn on November 21, 1975, two DC 4's were ready to take off from Iconi airport. They are in charge of the one hundred and fifty men that Ali Soilihi, convinced that the inhabitants of Mayotte are waiting for him like the Messiah persists in wanting to lead the peaceful march on Mayotte. While Yves Le Bret climbs into the first apparatus. Ali Soilihi takes me aside. 'When the planes have returned empty,' you won't send them back to Mayotte until I give you the order myself. Don't listen to anyone else. You will see that Mayotte, from tonight, will be

Comorian, even if I have to die for her (para 45)."

When the planes land at Dzaoudizi airport, Soilihi advances with his "Pink March" towards the French gendarmes with his mapinduzi (revolutionaries) and says "Mahorais, I have come as a friend to offer your dignity in Freedom (Denard, para 46)."

A crowd of mostly women jeer at the liberators and douse some with gasoline and threaten fire if they don't dispatch. Soilihi returns and marches his pinked scarved mapinduzi and declares Maores will join Comoros in due time.

On November 26th in response to French control and meddling, he seizes French administration property. In response, France recalls four hundred civil servants and gendarmes from Comoros. As Defense Minister, Soilihi also buys 300 hundred assault rifles, submachine guns, and pistols from unknown sources to defend the revolution.

Socialist Revolution, Mongozi Ali Soilihi, and the Social and Secular Republic

> *"The Third World must start over a new history of man 'for they are incubational moments (Gramsci cited in Fanon, 1967, xv)."*

"Citizens, do you know the enemies of the Comorian nation, citizens, do you know them? The first among the enemies of the Comorian nation is France, the French state. Citizens, let's stay calm, let's listen well. Our first enemy is France, it's the French state, it's not the French"\
---Ali Soilihi (Comoroes-Online.com).

If August 3, 1975, marks the breaking moment from French monopoly of the archipelago, then January 2, 1976, is when the institutional break was consummated. The election of the pair at the head of the State, Ali Soilihi by the National Council of State (CEN) and the Council National of the Revolution (CNR).

To Denard's own memoirs, it is outstanding on how Soilihi's revolutionary position was somehow unmasked when the revolutionary moment was nigh. Denard discusses this "unmasking" of Soilihi's "true nature" as the Mongozi Ali Soilihi discusses the future state of the armed forces:

> "As soon as he is in power, Ali Soilih reveals his true nature. After announcing that he was going to make a 'clean slate of the past," he disallowed the notion of Denard wanting to have Guineans in charge of the army. Denard writes that Soilihi says "I don't want to hear about an army structured on the colonial mode. We are living in a revolution, and a revolution does not need ranks! (Denard, year unknown, para 56)."

Ali Soilihi declares his intention to make a clean break from the past and rejects the idea put forth by Denard of having Guineans in charge of the army. Soilihi expresses his disdain for the colonial-era military structure, stating that he does not want an army organized according to colonial ranks. Instead, he emphasizes the revolutionary context in which they are living and asserts that a revolution does not require hierarchical ranks. This stance reflects Soilihi's commitment to revolutionary ideals and his desire to overhaul traditional power structures inherited from the colonial period.

To Mukonoweshuro (1990) aftermath of the coup demanded that the hierarchical system of sultans and French landed class be overthrown:

> "Ali Soilihi's immediate post-coup rhetoric had initially projected him as a man of the people, a visionary, determined to overthrow the traditional semi-feudal religious hierarchy that had been so influential in the islands even under French colonial rule (Mukonoweshuro,1990, p.568)."

Soilihi positioned himself as a champion of the common people, advocating for social justice and the dismantling of traditional power structures, including the influence of the semi-feudal religious hierarchy. Soilihi was left to create something new after others were knocked down by their own conflicts and power struggles.

The country was mostly agrarian and without industry of its own to form a highly advanced proletarian socialism advocated by Marx. With the inspiration of the Chinese Revolution basing their power on peasants and lumpenproletariat, the Comorian revolution would not base itself on the proletariat.

The Social Revolution that would obstinately be known as uniquely Soilihist and of Ali Soilihi's imagination would try to create socialism in the Comoros. This would include abolishing such customs as the wearing of veils, the costly grand marriage, traditional funeral ceremonies, abolish the civil service for Comorian citizens, the commanding heights of the economy nationalized, and power distributed to moudriyas, and the Moissey to defend the revolution.

It is ambiguous of who dismissed whom. Whether if Denard finding out Ali Soilihi's socialist inclinations, or if when Ali Soilihi learned that Denard was a mercenary working for the French capitalists. When Soilihi dismissed Denard, Denard reportedly says "I will come back, you'll see (Kweli,2024)!" Meaning, Denard had an inkling that the revolution would be overthrown by himself.

Ranger interviewing Soilihi asks about the future of the French government, independent Comoros, and liberation of Maore/Mayotte. Soilihi uses terms "abrupt break" from France and conservative traditions to describe the curtness and rapid need for socialism in Comoros as its next evolutionary stage:

> "The future unfortunately is quite dark. It is dark and not due to our fault, believe me. You know very well that the Comorian people has been a French colony for 150 years. There has never been bloodshed in this country. Evolution was always accomplished in a gentle fashion. We have gone through various phases of our political evolution, always in an amicable fashion. Today we suddenly have this abrupt break. If the future today is rather dark, then let the French Government not entertain any illusions the Comorian people is determined to liberate Mayotte. And I am not just talking for myself here. I

> only represent the people, and I am sure that I represent them. They are determined to liberate Mayotte regardless of the conditions. Now what will happen in the future I don't know. But the fact is that the Comorian people is determined to go all the way (Rangers, 1976, p. 5)."

Despite this uncertainty, Soilihi asserts the determination of the Comorian people to liberate Maore/Mayotte, a sentiment they claim to represent on behalf of the people. He makes it clear that this determination is unwavering, regardless of any conditions or obstacles. While unsure about what the future holds, Soilihi concludes by affirming the resolve of the Comorian people to pursue this goal with unwavering commitment.

In December 1975, the regime announced the promulgation of a Socialist Charter which was to provide guidelines for the overthrow of existing social, economic, religious, and political institutions. This onslaught on the prevailing patterns of societal organization was to be spearheaded by a newly created National Council of Institutions, replacing the National Revolutionary Council.

The new constitution abolished the existing government ministries and replaced the old colonial-style local government administration by a decentralized system controlled by presidential appointees (French, 1997). The old colonial-style local government administration was replaced by a centralized revolutionary system.

In this new system, control over local administration is shifted to presidential appointees, suggesting a centralization of power under the presidency.

This restructuring reflects a departure from the previous administrative framework and a move towards a more centralized governance structure.

Nouvelle Génération Soilihste, a contemporary revolutionary Soilihist youth group in Comoros and in France posted the entire Socialist Charter of Comoros which included solidarity with Global South movements, establishment of the social and secular republic, against superstition, and the fight against the many oppressions. The full Socialist Constitution is in the Appendix:

"The fight against disease, hunger, and ignorance:

- ➤ The struggle for the liberation and emancipation of women, peasant youth and Comorian workers. Administrative and political decentralization. "Where there are people, there is power"

- ➤ The permanent struggle for the reintegration of the Comorian island Mayotte. In the concerts of the Nations, France had several times used its right of veto at the UN. And to date, no country in the world has recognized the legitimacy of France on the Comorian island of Mayotte, to my knowledge. A country smaller than the city of Marseilles knew how to sensitize the world including the unconditional allies of France in the concerts of the Nations....

- ➤ The struggle for the establishment of a unitary and secular state.

- ➤ The fierce fight against corruption, the embezzlement of public funds.
- ➤ The support of all the peoples of the world who advocate and fight for their freedom and their independence: Palestine. Namibia. POLISARIO,

Rhodesia. South Africa. Latin and South American countries. etc.

➢ The struggle for the national unity of the Comorian people, in its diversity. Self-management of the islands:

➢ Strict application of positive neutralism. Against any foreign, extra-African military presence on Comorian soil. This is called positive non-alignment.

➢ Development and consolidation with neighboring countries of a policy of good neighborliness, peace, solidarity, friendship, and good South-South cooperation with brotherly and neighboring countries.

➢ The revalorization of the Comorian language, cultures, and specificity.

➢ The reform of the tradition in its practice, against the very useless ostentatious expenses which constitute an obstacle for the development of the Comorian and the country, by its gravity.

➢ Parity, protection, equality of men and women, the emancipation of the latter.

➢ The literacy of the population, (62% in 3 years). Only Nicaragua under Daniel Ortéga's Sandinistas has done better, (80% but in 5 years). (NGS-Nouvelle Génération Soilihste,2020)."

This constitution connects to previous revolutionaries and observes traditions that needed to be addressed and not ignored or erased when dealing with dialects, languages, and customs of Comoros. Furthermore, the preamble of the basic law written and created by Soilihi to the Comorian people in 1977's points were emphasized:

> ➤ Work is a right and obligation for all men and women who are not hindered by age or physical disability. The state therefore strives to promote full employment and ensure everyone's fair remuneration for their participation in production.

> ➤ In respect of the natural balances that condition their renewal, all natural resources of the Comoros, soil, subsoils, forests, seawater, and seabed, must be exploited to the best of the general interest. The right of property cannot in any way hinder this necessity.

> ➤ Equality of rights between men and women is agreed on both the civil and civic level, and on the effective plan of employment and opportunities for promotion.

> ➤ The Administration is at the service of manual workers and remains under their control. The cost of its operation, which is fatally deducted from the budgetary revenues allocated for productive investments, must be kept to a minimum.

> ➤ The Administration ensures only the essential services that cannot yet be provided by the manual workers themselves. The training of young people and adults is designed to guide all communities towards self-management (NGS-Nouvelle Génération Soilihiste,2020 website)."

Overall, these principles underscore the commitment of the new constitution to promoting social justice, sustainable resource management, gender equality, efficient governance, and community empowerment within the Comoros.

The country was renamed the Secular and Social Republic of Comoros. Full mobilization of the masses would promote food self-sufficiency, appropriate education, full employment, and health care. During this period, the village of Wani was chosen as a pilot city for the projects of the revolution in Ndzuani. The first administrative unit was the mourdiya, or equivalent to the soviet as in USSR.

Air Comores was nationalized in April 1977. Comoros was the only socialist country to legalize marijuana (French, 1997). Comoros' embrace of socialist principles during this period included state-led development initiatives, centralized governance structures, and progressive social policies.

The Mongozi Ali Soilihi knew that inequalities could only change and be transformed by a revolution of structures, mentalities, and institutions so that a new order would replace the old. He put in place a five-year development plan that would allow the emancipation of the Comorians. The regime proclaimed its commitment to the 'liberation' of women and the youth, who, it said, represented 52 per cent of the total population (Daou,2017, para 6)." The state would also commit itself to land reform as part of the socialist development.

One of the main impetuses of the revolution was agrarian reform and the distribution of land. It was to be planned that each of the islands would have certain sector cultivation areas, including soil maps to plant cassava, wheat, maize, and bananas (Bambao-RTV Mvouni-Bambao, 2015).

Every citizen was to be given a piece of land, ranging from one to two acres, and was to be legally bound to farm it. The development of market gardening particularly, the introduction of onions produced within the communal gardens and schools of the mouridays, as a major part of Soilihism (Giachino, 2005a).

The need to control one's destiny regarding agrarian is tied to the oppression of Comorians. Throughout the centuries, the islands were made to grow ylang-ylang, coffee, and other crops that were exported. The country would also try to rid itself of oppression superstitions that benefited the sultans and French neo-colonialism

Religion and Sorcery

"Soilihi said to young people: 'Get them out of the mosques. We jostled them a bit.'"
(Daou, 2017, p. 56).

Soilihi being an atheist Muslim, meant that the 'False religions' as Islams, were to be sidelined as a hegemonic power. Any attempt of historians to make Comorian socialist into an atheistic state is wrong. If there were such an attempt by Soilihi to do so would so, meaning to neutralize religiously inspired dissent, particularly Islamic dissent, would cause an outrage (Kweli, 2024).

However, the regime decreed a ban on some Islamic customs. Soilihi did not hide his distrust of the religious leaders whom he accused of using their knowledge to assert their superiority over socialism. But that was easier said than done.

Giachino writes that "Arabic was present in religious education, in informal schools, with Comorian remaining in the domain of oral communications, family correspondence, private manuscripts in Arabic characters or private law acts of cadis" (Giachino, 2005b, para 5).

Enforcing socialist secularism, the armed revolutionary militia, Moissey were allowed to attack religious institutions and customs.

Soilihi banned official religion but as an atheist Muslim, did not erase Islam from the state (Peterson, 2021, p. 18)." Soilihi's stance as an atheist Muslim who banned official religion while still acknowledging Islam's cultural and historical significance reflects a delicate balancing act. Despite officially separating religion from the state, Soilihi likely recognized the enduring influence of Islam in Comorian society and sought to navigate this reality without completely erasing it. This approach allowed him to maintain support from both secular and religious segments of the population while promoting a more inclusive and pluralistic vision of the state.

There is precedence to have a Muslim communist within the realm of international communist leaders and theoreticians. Sultan Galiev was a Muslim communist and participant in the Russian Revolution. Galiev's claim to fame was that exploited nations under the rule of European imperialism were "proletarian nations" and that are more oppressed than European workers.

As a theoretical example this means, as per Comorian workers, they do not own the means of production twice removed. The Comorian proletariat does not own local ylang-ylang fields nor the incipient factories that process the ylang-ylang nor the docks that transport it. As per Galiev, Comorian workers do not own the means of any apparatus of a united nation-state or apparatus due to being ruled by French imperialism (Beil, 2015).

This observation reflects a critique of the impact of colonialism and imperialism on the economic and political structures of the Comoros, emphasizing the need for liberation and self-determination.

Soilihi's willingness to move away from the deeply rooted Islamic heritage of the islands was viewed by many conservative and feudalistic elements as betrayal to the island's culture. Yet, the Comorian flag of the Soilihi period attempted to present a break from non-secular Islam yet make sure there was not a total erasure of Islam.

The red horizontal bar standing for the revolution was made larger and placed above the green bar that past and future flags used to represent Comoros' attachment to the colors of Islam (Daou, 2017). In the corner was a crescent moon connecting Islamic traditions, and four stars stood for all the Comorian islands.

Socialism radically differentiated from traditions that many Comorians consider integral to their identity as not only Muslims, but the specific traditions of Comorian Islam (Daou, 2017). The Socialist Charter made it clear that it would uphold democracy and socialism as the vanguard of idealism instead of superstition as an oppressive tool.

The Socialist Charter writes that: "The struggle for the defense of authentic Islam. Against witchcraft and charlatanism, against the use of Islam as an instrument of exploitation of the Comorian people" (NSG–Nouvelle Soilihist Generation).

This highlights a struggle within the Comorian society for the defense of authentic Islam against various perceived threats. These threats include witchcraft, charlatanism, and the exploitation of Islam as a tool for oppressing the Comorian people. This struggle underscores the desire to uphold the true principles and teachings of Islam while resisting practices and interpretations that are seen as detrimental or exploitative.

It suggests a broader social and cultural movement aimed at reclaiming and preserving the integrity of Islamic beliefs and practices, while also combating superstition and manipulation. This effort reflects a commitment to justice, authenticity, and empowerment within the context of religious identity and community values.

Soilihi banned organized sorcery as connection to the feudal leftovers. There has been rumors that Soilihi had his own private sorcerer helping him dictate events. However, there is no concrete evidence that he relied on his own sorcerer that told the Moissy to get rid of all the dogs on the islands (Ottenheimer & Ottenheimer,1994). But this myth happened as Denard brought a black dog as a superstitious *fait accompli* upon usurping Comorian socialism in 1978.

Archipelago-Unity and the Creation of the Nation-State

The days of Soilihist Comoros had the only three years of freedom, democracy, and self-agency in Comorian history. Historian of Comoros, Ian Walker seconds this regarding Comorian self-efficacy and writing that "more than anything else, however Comorians today remember this regime as the only one since independence that had a political project, and one that promoted a sense of national identity and true independence (Walker, 2019, p. 161)." This "political project" meant that it was the only regime with a sense of national characteristics in trying to undo colonial harm and trauma.

In "Apologists of Neo-Colonialism" written by the Chinese Communist Party, state support for revolutions in Africa, Asia, and Latin America (Alemayehu, 2020b) suggests that:

> "struggle waged by African revolutionary forces for democracy, be this within the framework of a general struggle for socialism or within limited perspectives, cannot revolve around a banal defense of democracy in general (Alemayehu, 2020b, paragraph, 5)."

It is in this political climate that Soilihi was inspired to get the "green light" indirectly towards a unique brand that became a nation-state of Comorian socialism.

Regarding policies of anti-feudalism and anti-imperialism, Ali Soilihi had faith in his ideas and revolutionary praxis but was fighting against what he thought against time. He knew that French forces would stop at nothing to end the progress of the state. Fighting on all fronts, at the head of the very young state, two questions essential interested him, in relatively Marxist terms:

1. The nationalization of the means of production and the organization of the commanding heights and management, the ways and means and everyday life.

2. The conflict and fight of conservative beliefs including conservative languages (Comoroes-Online.com, no year, para 57)."

To combat these beliefs, Soilihi, using the "language du verb," created and constructed a language for and from the masses, using Shikomori (a form of Swahili unique to the island of the archipelago) as a vessel.

Instead of the island differences, Ali Soilihi used to talk to people on every region. This reinforces the feeling and concept of archipelago unity and nation-state while making sure the noticed distance between islands. The distance was not measured by geographical, as per Comorians. He wanted to bring the islands together regarding all the differences in language dialects.

"The desire to wipe the slate clean was intimately linked to the irreversible nature of the revolutionary project" (Comoroes-Online.com, no year, para 57).

There was a real desire, like all revolutionary socialist states in the 20th century, to engage in *tabula rasa*.

Ali Soilihi was concerned about the fragile union regarding the other islands. After the attempted island separation in 1997 and 2006 he reinforces himself as a prophet. Seeing a sense of island-hood versus archipelago-hood, a member of the Moissy says that "I feel Anjouanese before feeling Comorian" -, he would have issued a warning against "the danger for the National Union", which "will come from Ndzuani" ... (Comoroes-Online.com, no year, para 78)."

Soilihi did not want the archipelago to splinter into successionist territories nor to keep Maore/Mayotte in French hands. PASCO regional secretary Salim Djabir of

Mwali/Mohelia said "We played a role in everything that was done, at least at the beginning and in the middle of the regime", Ali Soilihi pushed for a union of all the islands. Hit hard by the French secession of Maore/Mayotte, Soilihi believed that centralization was "the antidote" to separatist desires.

Propaganda for the Masses

> "Become literate now"
> -Comorian socialist slogan (Comoroes-Online.com)

> "Excuse me, but now you have to become literate! "
> -Ali Soilihi (Giachino,2005a, para 6)."

ThThe first independent newspaper in Comoros, *Courier de Comores*, was published in 1976 by a *Figaro*-trained journalist, Hadji Hassanali. It was a four-page tabloid, printed in Tanzania's commercial capital Dar es Salaam. After seeing his first two issues dominated by government-sponsored articles on the Marxist concept of history, Hassanali fled the country and ended his paper's publication.

Besides *Courier de Comores*, only pamphlets and political tracts dominated Comoros' media landscape (Onyango-Obbo, 2021). PASOCO had its newspaper entitled *Uhuru* (Independence). This reformist Marxist paper was distributed at least five hundred copies per week, pushing for independence and the end of the Grande Marriages (Ottenheimer & Ottenheimer, 1994).

The emergence of independent newspapers in Comoros, albeit short-lived and often constrained by government influence, represented important steps towards a more pluralistic media environment and the promotion of freedom of expression in the country.

Beholden to the legacy of the socialist Comoros, the radio workers, spokespersons, journalists were indeed the collective memory of the revolutionary experience that continues to this day. Journalist Said Hassane Jaffar with Radio Comores at the time acknowledges that there is disinformation from many journalists, historians, and primary documents regarding the socialist Comoros (Abdoul-Djabar and Zakaria, 2021). Said Hassane Jaffar's acknowledgment of disinformation surrounding the socialist Comoros reflects the complexity of historical narratives and the challenges of accurately documenting past events, especially in politically charged contexts. The socialist period in Comoros was marked by ideological divisions, political repression, and competing interpretations of history, leading to differing accounts from journalists, historians, and primary documents.

Radio was the main source of mass propaganda during the revolution. A committee called "Broadcasting Care (in Swahili "Utrangazaji Ulezi") had the responsibility of creating religious, public health, and cultural health programs. Interviewed 43 years after the death of Ali Soilihi and the revolution, radio spokespersons Touma Bacary, Faouzia Ali Amir, and Mohamed Mzé, Irahim Ahmada Koutub. discuss the importance of radio at the time. Radio interviews presented many problems regarding the daily life of revolutionary struggle. They discuss how Ali Soilihi and the

Soilihist revolution took to radio against illiteracy (Abdoul-Djabar & Zakaria, 2021).

Fundi Mzé Mohamed discussed how as general manager of Radio Comores, the purposes of the radio broadcasts were not presenting empty hyperbole, but to encourage food production, revolutionary esprit d'corps, and nutrition:

"The objective of this communication was to popularize the development plan and the interim objectives. The main goal of the diet was food self-sufficiency. We had to encourage food crops through awareness raising, sensitization, popularization, through our broadcasts. During the Solihist (Authors Note) revolution, the radio was not used to make praises as some may have thought (Abdoul-Djabar & Zakaria, 2021, para 8)."

The communication strategy outlined in the quote aimed to popularize the development plan and interim objectives among the population. One of the primary goals emphasized was the promotion of food crops to achieve food self-sufficiency. To achieve this objective, the radio was utilized for awareness-raising, sensitization, and popularization efforts. Rather than serving as a platform solely for praising the regime, the radio was employed as a means of disseminating important information and mobilizing the population towards specific developmental goals, such as increasing agricultural productivity and reducing dependency on external food sources.

This is important to note that before the revolution there was no daily on-the-ground communication between the masses. Socialist radio was used to be a helpful conduit towards humanist progression. To solve the problem of the revolutionary radio, a participant of the revolution said:

> "Ali Soilihi Mtsashiwa had set up committees in the other islands which served as relays for the transmission of messages. He only knew the essential points of his speech and had this gift of transmitting his message as if he had it before his eyes. Soilihi tried to make communication a lever for development" because transparent and popular communication is the way for a revolution to succeed (Abdoul-Djabar & Zakaria, 2021, para 9)."

Soilihi's approach to communication underscores its central role in driving social and political transformation. By leveraging communication as a means of mobilization, coordination, and transparency, he sought to advance his revolutionary goals and bring about meaningful change in the Comoros. Mohamed Mze describes that the 24-hour radio program contributed to the day's happenings to the Comorian population. Mze writes in an interview decades later regarding what programs the masses were more respondent to:

> "[w]e found, in particular, the national committee, the regional committees whose role was not only to transmit the message to the population but also to inform the president on what is happening in the country (Abdoul-Djabar & Zakaria, 2021, para 4)." Thus, the regional committees

and national committee confirmed that radio was a key asset to delivering programs and information to the three islands.

Regarding Ali Soilihi's direct influence on and use of radio, ex-"Moissy" member Ibrahim Ahamada Koutoub spoke of Soilihi and the importance of radio as the "centerpiece of his action (Abdoul-Djabar & Zakaria,2021, para 7)." Specialists coordinating legal information and culture kept Soilihi connected to the other islands and the centralization of radio became ever so critical because "{t}his is why there were specialists from different fields: coordination, legal, cultural (Abdoul-Djabar & Zakaria,2021, para 7)." Not only did radio keep all the islands connected, but for specific purposes. For Faouzia Ali Amir, a young journalist of Radio Comoros, says that Ali Soilihi considered the radio to be an indispensable tool for "making the revolution triumph", with one program subtitled "Informing and unveiling the ideals of popular Mongozi politics (Abdoul-Djabar & Zakaria,2021, para 7)."

Radio Comores tried to create working conditions that were up to standard. Soilihi prioritized radio as a crucial platform. These programs, including a theater program, address topics like early marriages, delinquency, and violence prevention, contributing to public education and awareness. Amir continues to say that "I joined Radio Comores, I was working in the editorial department. The working conditions met the standards. For the president, radio was a top priority. We had several programs, including a theater program that educated the population on early marriages, delinquency, and the fight against violence, among other things (Abdoul-Djabar & Zakaria,2021 para 9)."

Ali Soilihi wanted to be able to coordinate as easily as possible the conditions of the revolution. From the use of radio, "the comrade president knew how to impose his popular and revolutionary policy on the population. In the event of a technical or other fault, they was the first to inform those responsible. I experienced it when I made a mistake when advertising a newspaper in French. The president called my superiors who interrupted the broadcast (Abdoul-Djabar & Zakaria,2021, para 11)."

Ali Soilihi had a very hands-on approach to Radio Comores at implementing his popular and revolutionary policies among the population. He took egalitarian approach in addressing technical or other issues, often being the first to inform those responsible and learn from their mistakes.

Specifically, how the radio was run, Papa Djambae (Abdoul-Djabar & Zakaria, 2021) writes specificalities regarding the communication teams and committees regarding that "[t]he Mongozi had set up three communication teams which ensured popular communication. The radio at the time only had an awareness-raising role focused on the importance of its new vision" for revolution.

Off the air, the regional committees were the first to convey the revolutionary initiatives that will be transmitted on the radio. Furthermore, there "were three teams. One in charge of the revolutionary theater, another of the chronicle" and the other on the presidential palace (para 17)."

Radio connected the Mongozi to the masses personally to the day-to-day revolution.

Besides radio, speeches were given in-person to galvanize the masses and fuse with Ali Soilihi's revolutionary struggle. Soilihi is shown as the limited footage of the time, in makeshift buildings discussing the revolution while people are reading up on policies. Even though limited, there is much video and photographic evidence of Soilihi being the on-the-ground orator and leader. Part of Soilihi's custom was that:

> "[he] traveled the country, to explain, as a good orator, the new practices to be put in place. He intended to reshape the landscape by establishing better relations between administrators and citizens. With this structure, it is the state administration that comes to the citizens, and not the other way around. This completely upsets the Comorian, who has always seen the administration as a power to which he had to submit. As a member of the Moissey, Koutoub concludes on Soilihi mass speeches for popular appeal. He (author's note: Ali Soililhi) had this aura and a natural ability to convey his messages in Shikomori. He avoided using French

> words or expressions as much as possible. It was, for him, a way of allowing citizens to quickly grasp his speeches (Giachino,2005a, para 6)."

Mass communication from newspapers to radio, to on-the ground guidance was central for the three islands to be aware of local and international events. The aura of Soilihi's popular appeal and oratory skills were never lost of the working masses that kept the Comorian revolution alive. Another function of the revolution was to organize literacy campaigns and schools.

Revolutionary Education Schools and Literacy Campaign

Despite monetary problems caused by historic French capitalism, the Comorian revolution opened fifty new secondary schools in less than three years. The problem of language vis-à-vis French versus the many dialectics of Shikimori-Comorian and Arabic became a major concern for the revolution (Walker, 2019).

The promotion of the use of Latin script to write Comorian was for practical reasons only, since typewriters produced at that time were not produced in Arabic script. Soilihi integrated Koranic and secular education in the curriculum to break from traditions of colonialism.

Regarding schools, there was some conflict between the role of education. The committees or the Mourdiya:

> " have not played the role assigned to them but house primary and secondary schools. The Comoros also owe the president the massive education of both girls and boys: it was Soilihi who decided to no longer limit the number of students admitted to sixth grade (Giachino,1998, para 8)."

Expanding access to education, especially at the secondary level, is crucial for the overall development of a nation. By removing restrictions on enrollment, more students, regardless of their gender, socioeconomic background, or other factors, can have the opportunity to pursue further education. This move aligns with efforts to improve literacy rates, promote gender equality, and foster human capital development in Comoros.

Basically, thinks Damir (2009), "the general literacy campaign was not his (author's note: Ali Soilihi) primary objective. He wanted to give an education to the committees and to the soldiers who were the spearhead of his revolution, and who were not educated" (para 34).

The educational reform also tackled problems which arise today regarding investment in schools. Dini Nassur, a former member of the National Committee writes that Soilihi called on Belgian and Canadian language experts to develop a more useful system to Comorian relatives:

> "The primary school had to integrate manual work, preparing the children to follow professional training in alternation

> to pass a technical Baccalaureate, then possibly to continue a training outside. The objective was simple: at all times, the student should be able, if he left school, to integrate professionally and be useful to society (Giachino,2005a, para 7)"

Soilihi's approach emphasizes the importance of practical skills and vocational training in preparing students for future success in the workforce. It acknowledges the diverse talents and aspirations of students and seeks to provide them with the necessary tools and opportunities to thrive in their chosen professions.

Dossar writes regarding a post-Revolutionary socialist Comores: "[a]fter 30 years, wouldn't we have been able to consolidate the training of technicians capable of stimulating local development?" (Giachino, 2005a, para 8).

Possible factors contributing to this perceived lack of progress could include insufficient investment in education and vocational training, limited access to resources and opportunities for technical skill development, as well as challenges related to political instability or economic constraints.

There were many years of French colonialism and Comorian capitalism that did not allow education and self-fulfillment through literacy. Right after the revolution, literacy became a priority and not only education of class-consciousness, and Marxism, but how ideologically language was a vital factor in decolonization.

Language of Ideology

Soilihi did not want to use French because it was the language of the oppressor. The revolution in Comoros was essentially creating a revolution of language. The language to be spoken as a united nation-state was "Comorian" - a dialect of Kiswahili, the Arabic-based lingua franca of East Africa - and, naturally, have also been strongly influenced by the French in matters of custom and language. Like Sankara and many other revolutionary Africans, it can be suggested that Soilihi used, like Otayek writes in Peterson (2021) "revolution du verbe": innovations in political discourse with rhetorical, symbolism, and storytelling, in easy understand Comorian language, religions, and superstitious tones It was education as a "language du verb", that Giachino writes the necessity to promote Shikomori versus French:

> "It was precisely to these young people that the president addressed himself in March 1976, insisting on the practical usefulness he intended to derive from the use of Shikomori: "How do we make a report? Study how to write it in Comorian in Arabic script, because there are people who don't know how to write French; study how to translate legal terms into Comorian, so that each of you who will be in a village, when he draws up a report to send it to court, knows how to do it in French or in Comorian(Giachino,2005a, para 6)."

This undoing of the oppressor language or the keeping of it was an extraordinary problem. In 1975 before the revolution, linguist Mohamed Ahmed Chamanga says that the "French alone was the language of public education and administration, which led to the exclusion of the greatest number of the march of the State" (Giachino, 2005a, para 6).

Soilihi wanted to prevent youth identifying with the non-secular Arabic world yet "the Arabic script would have required the use of letters from Comorian society. There is an ideological capital invested in the Arabic script, it's a whole universe: we identify it with a language, a religion, a tradition..." (Giachino, 2005a, para 6).

Language plays a crucial role in shaping cultural identity and fostering a sense of belonging to a nation-state.

Linguistic policies under Soilihi functioned as instruments of ideological formation, positioning language as a medium through which socialist nation-building could be enacted. By privileging linguistic frameworks, these policies sought to consolidate Comoros' diverse population within a unified national identity, thereby aligning cultural cohesion with the broader project of socialist statecraft.

Regarding Afrocentricity and language, Ali Soilihi continued to perpetuate the Swahili language, which is spoken in 14 East African countries (Roinka, 2020). By promoting Swahili, Soilihi may have sought to create a sense of linguistic unity among the people of Comoros and across East Africa. This emphasis on linguistic and cultural solidarity aligns with the principles of Afrocentricity and may have contributed to efforts to build a stronger sense of African identity and collective consciousness.

Other deeper motivations probably also explain why the president favored this option. Ali Soilihi wanted to have the revolution deliberately be a youth revolution who can break with the past using Latin characters more easily, to ensure literacy.

Damir Ben Ali (2009) was astounded by the transcription of Shikomori being developed by Soilihi. Damir Ben Ali writes regarding this that "he told me that I had to work first with the committees [political committees made up of very young activists, Author's note]. There are members of the committee who proposed letters that he adopted, such as the 'v' which was written 'pv.' I was confused. In our first conversation, it was a question of teachers" (Gitchino 2009, para 23)!

Ben Ali's confusion about the nature of his initial conversation with Soilihi highlights the complexity of the language and education initiatives being discussed. The shift from discussing teachers to linguistic matters reflects the multifaceted nature of Soilihi's agenda and the interconnectedness of language, education, and political activism in his vision for societal transformation which has changed generations of Comorians.

In a blog post called *"Ali Soilihi, Maker of the Imagination"*, it discusses an article regarding Comorian identity and language. The language use gave Comorian feeling of value (Eku, 2004). Many vocabularies were created and are propagated in the contemporary era. Many words and expressions were brought out of the shadows by Ali Soilihi and now passed into common language.

An article originally published in *Kashkazi* No. 7 writes that the language was greatly enriching. Damir Ben Ali writes that "[we] were preparing lists of political vocabulary, of which the Comorian language was very poor at the time. They were sent on the radio, and they were displayed on a board" (para 7).

The nuance of the revolution was to overcome and vanquish traditional language through hermeneutics to ensure that the revolution was to make the divide from an oppressive past.

The action to push the masses writing and working in Shikomori when the bourgeoise and French imperialists wrote and worked in French is very real. Shikomori was highly segregated based on regional dialects and class.

Damir Ben Ali (2009) writes that "[t]here was a Comorian language of the great educated notables that people of lower level did not understand. Peasants and fishermen had their own language" (para 23).

To create new identity, and new administration, and new media, Soilihi tried to unify the language. Michel Lafon states that "to express oneself in Grand Comorian meant including the language in the global project of revolutionary change: even if, no doubt, Grand Comorian had already been used in local political debate (...) it is Ali Soilihi who made him reach the national level suddenly" (Giachino, 1998, para 7).

Trying to create a proletarian socialist language and overturn language normalcies right away was daunting at best, especially when it came to regional and island dialects.

Opponents of Ali Soilihi claim that he used revolutionary language and wanted to create a revolutionary language for people that were pushed into a scenario that was an anti-thesis of their language customs. From Soililhi's experience from being part of the class struggle in France regarding public speaking, Soilihi draws on his exceptional knowledge of Comorian populist mentalities of which to organize an orally based tradition.

"He would look in the mental representations of the Comorian to express his modern conception"-writes linguist Mlaïli Condro. The Mongozi Ali Soilihi not only wanted to use dialectical and ... localism to usurp imperialism. Through the word of power, Soilihi gave them all the semantic amplitude which is that of a concept (Giachino,2005a, para 9)."

Soilihi provides revolutionary linguistics from regional vocabulary, updating and providing from old words as resource for his "revolution du verbe." For this "revolution du verbe," Soilihi takes expressions and vernaculars from Swahili, Arabic, and even French.

Explains Ahmed Chamanga that Soilihi "tried to follow the same policy as that practiced in Tanzania with Swahili: for borrowings, first started by looking at regional varieties, then close at neighboring languages, then Arabic and finally European languages" (Giachino, 2005a, para 9).

To confuse the already confusion of Comorian local dialectics, class dialectics, and localisms, the language had more Swahili than what was known as Comorian. Using Latin script and not Arabic to dictate Shikomori for purposes of transcribing was needed imperatively.

Damir Ben Ali was called on by Soilihi for supervision regarding this creation of revolutionary language. Ben Ali said that: "he (Soilihi) called me and told me about his project; we had agreed that we were going to do it in Arabic characters. At the time, the literacy rate in Latin characters was only 23%, whereas if we adopted Arabic characters, almost the entire population would benefit. But when I came back to see him, everything was turned upside down" (Giachino, 2005b, para 9).

Trying to create a centralized language based on localism proved more difficult than realized. Technology aggravated the process as well. Since there were no typewriter machines with Arabic characters, some printed propaganda was helped with Tanzanian advisors. Tanzania uses Latin script for Swahili transcription. Ahmed Chamanga presents this as positive happening because "Latin characters are easier to adapt to render the sounds of the Comorian language, while Arabic characters would require the creation of many additional diacritical marks, therefore not available on typewriters (Giachino,2005b para, 7)." Also because of the possibility of having two writing scripts one in Arabic and another in French, would bring impossible problems to everyday life in the Social and Secular Republic.

To Soilihi's ex-linguistic advisor Damir Ben Ali, the linguistic policy achieved two legacy phenomena. Many words and phrases continue to this day brought on by Soilihism. Regarding how the program worked, "[t]owards the end, he isolated himself. He had surrounded himself with children who accepted what he said but who no longer brought him anything. From April 1977, these young people occupied the radio and used a language which did not please people very much. There was a devaluation of the Comorian language (Giachino, 1998, para 6). "The case of letting the revolutionary youth be the vanguard while legitimizing the language of the oppressor seem too much, but nor was it delegitimating the revolution. Ahmed Chamanga reinters that:

> "[t]he teaching of a language and its use cannot be improvised. We had to prepare them. What did we have at the time? No description of the language, no human resources capable of providing the necessary training... The consequences of

> this hasty approach were random spelling, and the production of documents that were difficult for linguists to use (Giachino, 1998, para 7)."

Not only did the ideological language try to spawn a class-conscious proletarian mindset, and engineer the soul of the youth, but art also was a main instigator of propaganda. The revolutionary youth was to be the vanguard regardless of language they spoke, their mission was to make the break from French capitalism and colonialization. The use of Shikomori was banned when Admed Abdallah came back to power after destroying the Social and Secular republic in 1978. Not till 1992 was Shikomori made and recognized as an official language.

Youth and Revolutionary Art

> " Love each other in the islands to have equality! Let's fight capitalism! Let's fight ignorance! (Verin,1994)."

The revolution inspired the young poets to be the many spokespersons of revolution, writing on themes of independence and sovereignty, and equality. Many poems concerned the fundamental themes of the Soilihist revolution regarding the state, the citizen, and the individual. The collective of the state, the conscious citizen, and the individual rights regarding creativity are what the revolution tried to defend.

The most frequent themes in this collection are revolution, independence, the unity of the archipelago, the Comorian nation, equal opportunities, food self-sufficiency, racial and island segregation, manual labor, and the enemies of the nation. There are also advertising themes on tourism, the fauna and flora, the coast, the landscape, and the environment, and the natural hospitality of the Comorians.

In short, the poetic themes chosen reflect this era of freedom in a newly independent country and this new revolutionary politics (Verin, 1994). The choice of poetic themes in the advertising campaign adds an element of artistic expression and emotional resonance. Poetic language can evoke a sense of wonder and inspiration, inviting travelers to immerse themselves in the beauty and cultural richness of Comoros.

Two other major factoring themes of the revolutionary Comorian poetry in the years of 1975-1978: were independence and revolution. These words was the watchwords of the Comorians who aspired to freedom. Some poets based on their inspiration on Comorian proverbs for song for revolutionaries regarding the Mongozi reminding them to achieve unity of the archipelago requires hard work. An example of this is poetry is that: " Everyone must do their part to succeed in the agrarian revolution (Verin,1994, p. 2)." Young poets and cultural activists paved the way for independence and individualism within the liberated spaces of the archipelago. All these changes as per these socio-economic initiatives were well received by the population, especially by these youth who, to assert their patriotism and nationalism, went as far as to transform the old name of the local orchestra.

It was the Comorian masses who requested the change of name by nationalizing the orchestra during a competition organized by the revolutionary power in Moroni in 1976 for the choice of the national anthems. (Verin,1994). The decision of the Comorian masses to nationalize the local orchestra and rename it during a competition for the national anthems illustrates the grassroots involvement in shaping cultural symbols and expressions. This act of renaming the orchestra reflects a desire to align cultural institutions with the revolutionary values of independence and sovereignty, further solidifying the connection between cultural identity and political ideology.

But as per Abu Chihabi's account, Ali Soilhi and he had discussed this proposal when Chihabi did not apply to the contest:

"When Ali (Soilhi) had the bright idea of organizing a competition for the composition of the national anthem, I did not find it relevant to take part. Many compositions were submitted to him. At the end of their listening, he exclaimed, surprised: " I did not hear Abu Chihabi 's proposal. » He was informed that I had not composed anything. He then ordered someone to come and get me immediately.

Maalesh 's younger son approached, shouting: "Abou, hide! Soldiers have come to take you away! Taken aback, I wondered if I had recently written a song criticizing the regime or something anti-revolutionary. But no, I hadn't done anything like that. So, I decided to confront them. My friends tried to dissuade me, but I joined them. The soldiers invited me to get into the back of the vehicle. As soon as we started, I asked for the window to be rolled down so everyone could see me leave. I heard a few people whisper: 'Abou harohorwa.' I was taken directly to the president's office. Courteously, he invited me to sit down and inquired about the reason for my non-participation in the national anthem contest. I explained to him that I did not have a tape recorder to record my composition. Less than ten minutes later, a man brought a tape recorder. I took it and left. I first went to the

Zawiani to pray, before going to the Baumer stadium. In the center of the field, I imagined the Comoros welcoming the whole world to the football World Cup, all the anthems blaring, ours closing the show. I then took out my guitar and started improvising a melody and the first lyrics.

Later, I made a model which I played to Ali. He listened attentively, asking to hear it again. Absorbed by the music, he lost himself in thought as he stared out the window at the scenery. When the song ended, tears rolled down her cheeks. I told him of my wish to refine the work and to solicit contributions from national musical associations to complete it. Seduced by this proposal, I received numerous suggestions from the four corners of the country which inspired me to compose the final anthem.

Ultimately, it was the people who contributed to the creation of this anthem. I brought together musicians and singers from various backgrounds to perform it as a choir. After several rehearsals, we recorded it at Radio Comoros. On Independence Day that year, we performed it at Independence Square in front of a huge crowd loving freedom and patriotism, just before Ali's much-anticipated speech, which was followed by of a concert with my band (Abu Shihabi cited in Kweli,2024)."

The collaborative and celebratory spirit surrounding the creation and performance of the national anthem of Comoros, emphasizes the anthem's role as a unifying symbol that embodies the shared values and aspirations of the people. These liberatory cultural aspects of poetry and song took place in the mouridayas, the administrative units that organized daily life on the ground. Without these mouridays, culture and communication would not flourish during the revolution.

Dietsche

Power to the Mourdiyas!

"Instead, we have decided to describe the kind of tabula rasa which from the outset fines any decolonization (Fanon,1967, p. 1)."

To connect government, land reform, and distribution of policies, the most important unit of popular mass expression and will was the mouridyas. Mouridyas (also spelled *Mudria*) would be one of the key structures and legacies of Solihism.

The government would be localized, establishing thirty-four mouridyas, or communal provinces. These would serve not only as administrative centers but would also provide post and telephone service for localities of about 9,000 people, modeled after the Chinese people's communes and workers' soviets of the USSR.

The mouridya would bring basic public services: civil status, justice, repression of fraud, health, education. The mouridyas, organized by peasants themselves, provided a local place to bring crops to market for the collective warehouses. The mouridyas provided the local support of the government and market center for the revolution.

The mouridya is both a political and administrative center, part of a form of centralization, allowing the citizen to be a real and concrete actor in the political, economic, cultural, judicial, informative, and social life of his commune.

Soilihi had introduced stabilized stone bricks for the annexes of the mouridya. These same bricks are reused today, especially on the island of Mohéli/Mwali.

Before the revolution, the peasants would have to include transportation to get the crop to Moroni, no matter what island they were on (country-data.com). To connect the mouridyas centers, "(Soilihi) traced all the roads, not only between the villages but also towards the places of production. He also developed the means of transport, in particular maritime" (Giachino, 2005a, paragraph 45).

Roads and superstructure were part of the huge understanding of socialist Comoros being made into a huge construction project.

The moudirya therefore tried to put an end to the imbalance at all levels, consisting in concentrating the administrative services in two large cities on each island, by helping the citizens of the other cities to constantly move about in their relationship to the state administration.

The great civil servants, often from the feudal bourgeoisie, only favored the facilities of the city, from which they came. The communities tried to undergo rapid socialization and stop reactionary competing positions of "our mourdiya against their mourdiya." This is also the reason the mourdiyas were installed between two towns, on "neutral" land for the most part.

Construction of superstructure would allow the citizens to take over the management of the city, getting used to another form of governance, to the point of understanding that they are and must be the strong link in the political, economic, cultural, and social life of his country. Lenin wrote that the Soviets were made so a cook could take over state government. This is no different than the Comorians and mouridiya. The "murdir" mentioned below is a type of commissar:

> "When these Mourdiya buildings are completed, the population will have at their disposal a judge (to arbitrate disputes), a nurse watching over a small popular pharmacy, a rudimentary slaughterhouse (and, one day, a cold room powered by a generator), a workshop-garage to maintain vehicles, an office responsible for coordinating basic education, a store to store the products collected, all under the authority of a mudir / first appointed by the Board of State, then elected by the population (Kweli, 2018, para 6)."

The mourdiya was a comprehensive and deliberate effort to address a broad spectrum of community needs, extending beyond basic services to encompass healthcare, education, and infrastructure maintenance. Such provisions suggest an integrated approach to development, where social welfare, knowledge production, and material sustainability were treated as interconnected domains essential to the well-being of the population. By embedding these facilities within the fabric of daily life, the state not only provided practical resources but also reinforced its role as the central guarantor of collective progress and stability.

So much that the revolution and mourdiya were known that even in contemporary times, the mourdiya were sung about. In the band awana *Afrobeat* the song "Mourdiya (tribute to Ali Soilihi) plays with visual clips of Mongozi as well as with other African liberation fighters such as Sankara, Kwame Nkrumah, and Patrice Lumumba. The song is also interspersed with Mongozi's speeches (Mawana Afrobeat, 2008). The use of visual clips allows the audience to connect more deeply with the historical context and the individuals being referenced in the song. This song also includes Mongozi's speeches within the song could serve to highlight his ideology, vision, and contributions to the liberation struggle. Additionally, in the appendix there are clips from a documentary showing the agrarian work within in a mouridiya (Appendix C).

Days of Ylang-Ylang Socialism

> "Socialism cannot be decreed from above...rejects the mechanical bureaucratic approach; living, creative socialism is the product of the masses themselves (Lenin,1917, para 23)."

On April 12, 1977, it is known that Soilihi dissolved the civil service and burnt centuries worth of French documents. The reason for this is that the civil service cost too much to run, taking up the whole public expenditure budget. Quickly, 3,500 civil servants out of 5,000 were dismissed. This measure, coupled with the earlier dismissal of French cooperants, tried to undo years of French influence and imperialism.

Ali Soilihi denounced the budget-intensive and inefficient public service inherited from colonization. Ex-activist Mohamed Dossar writes that "[we] pay 80% of state revenue for not much, since the civil servants, poorly paid, are not motivated" (Giachino, 2005d, para 4).

The dissolution of the civil service had the merit of considering the realities of the country. Dossar writes that Ali Soilihi "wanted to do a small but quality public service, with technicians" (Giachino, 2005d, para 5).

The dissolution of the civil service signaled a departure from the past and an attempt to address the realities of the country. Soilihi aimed to establish a leaner, more efficient public service that focused on quality rather than quantity. According to Dossar, Soilihi envisioned a smaller but highly skilled workforce, consisting of technicians and specialists rather than a bloated bureaucracy.

There are great parallels of action against bureaucracy and the French civil service. In Maoist-inspired terms, instead of "bombarding the headquarters," the Comorian socialist way was to get rid of the headquarters. Soilihi said in speech "Citizens, we were set for a transitional period of five weeks that is, thirty-five days since the abolition of the civil service, this great legacy of French colonialism, a major handicap in the life of Comorian workers (Walker,2009, p.2)." The decision to abolish the civil service represents a revolutionary break from the past and a rejection of the systems and institutions that perpetuated colonial domination. Soilihi's reference to a "transitional period of five weeks" underscores the urgency and decisiveness with which his administration sought to implement radical reforms and chart a new course for the country.

Overall, the Maoist-inspired rhetoric and actions employed by Soilihi and his administration reflect a commitment to revolutionary change and the dismantling of colonial legacies in pursuit of socialist ideals and national liberation. Ali Soilihi gave a speech to high school students in Mutsamudu regarding the decision of the destruction of the bureaucratic civil service:

> "It should be remembered that the cost of the functioning of our entire administration during these last years and more particularly during the year 1975 amounted to some 8 billion CFA Francs. I say the functioning of our administrative system, that is to say exclusively of any investment, except for this

expenditure amounting to 8 billion CFA francs, the Comorian part itself barely reaches 2 billion, that means comrade that if we have chosen and in fact I am going to say that if we go back on our political options and that we think it necessary to maintain the same level of our administration, the same operating system and the same expenditure structures, we will therefore have to find something share some 6 to 7 billion since this sum is missing. So, a first dilemma, should we keep our administrative system as it works and in which case, we will have to go travel the world, reach out and get these six billion that we are missing. And are there countries that are available to give the Comorian State 6 billion a year so that this State can ensure the level of functioning of its administration. And how many states would even be available? So, comrades, what will independence be worth in this case! Because we know that in a household when the working husband and wife earn 20,000 per month and they spend 50,000 fc during this month then the independence of the household is threatened and for the country it's the same thing (Walker,2019, p. 67)."

All civil servants, except for those operating essential services, were dismissed and existing files and dossiers were burned. On the independent islands, Soilihi introduced radical changes, centralizing the administration, and embarking on a process of nationalization and land reform. For the first time an attempt was being made both to authentically Comorianize the state and to develop a sense of national identity by totally breaking from the past. There is speculation that the abolishing of civil service and records was to retaliate against French support for Maore/Mayotte. By abolishing the civil service and destroying French government archives, Soilihi may have sought to send a strong message of defiance to France and assert Comoros' sovereignty over its territories. The destruction of records related to Maore/Mayotte could be interpreted as a symbolic act of rejecting French colonialism and asserting Comorian identity and independence (Walker,2019). Yet, there is evidence, that Ali Soilhi intoned a showmanship and that he never had all the French civil documents burned. As per Kwali (2024):

> "I know it's something his opponents often criticize him for, but based on my extensive investigations, it seems that Ali enjoyed staging events to leave a lasting impression. On that day, it was a symbolic gesture to break away from the colonial system. Abdoulwahab, whose memoirs I am currently working on, and who was the head of the central committee, told me that Ali asked him to go and safeguard the archives and to only take a few unimportant papers to burn them symbolically, marking the break from the old colonial regime (Kwali, 2024j, email)."

This suggests that Soilihi was aware of the symbolic significance of the act and intended it to serve as a statement of independence and liberation from colonial influence. While some may criticize Ali Soilihi for such theatrical displays, it seems that his intention was to make a bold statement and to cement his administration's commitment to breaking away from the old colonial regime and establishing a new order based on independence and self-determination.

The Grande Marriages and the liberation of Gender

Gender liberation was key to the revolution's success and the Grande Marriages are a major feudal concept that an obstacle to this success. Abolishing the Grande Marriages was a key part of the socialist revolution that ended matrilocal polygyny. Very much how it parallels with pre-revolutionary Comoros, Mao discusses how the "four authorities of "political, clan, religious, and masculine, -are the embodiment of the whole feudal-patriarchal ideology and system... (Mao, 1961, p.294)." One of the critiques by bourgeoise writers, academics, and Comorian politicians is the breaking up of these "Grande marriages" in the socialist society destroyed organized religion and tradition with Islam.

One of the most reactionary ways that the sultan and feudal system oppresses gender that has continued for many decades is. "Matrilocal polygyny". A married man having several wives would be unthought of at the time. But unlike bigamy, there is a rotation system of the husband with each of his wives in residence (Walker,2019). Yet, he treats each household in an equitable manner, even though despite the fact that this is a mini form of communal patriarchy. The husband during a period of time lives in each household with distance as the dependent factor.

Wedding ceremonies were based on what position the husband was in related to feudal society. The household was supposed to be seen as equals, but class in relation to sultan-patriarchy, it is explicitly a male-dominated arrangement (Walker, 2019). The first marriage was a relatively large public ceremony whereas the second and subsequent marriages were smaller.

Before the Berlin Conference, there was an opportunity for husbands and wives to be part of the Indian Ocean trade. Marriage also created social status, freedom, power, and wealth not attained in pre-capitalist and capitalist underdevelopment colonized societies (Ottenheimer, H., Ottenheimer, M., 1994b). The more time is spent in the household depends on how further apart the married man is from the wife-household.

> "Aturia," a student at the time, regards that the Grande Marriages are: "…bad thing since we live in an underdeveloped country. We build huge houses, we spend crazy sums for the big wedding, while next door, people have nothing to eat! The great marriage destroys the economy of the country. In a family, a person prefers to keep his money for marriage rather than pay for school for the children, give them food properly, offer them a good life! It is a challenge for the future, the great marriage" (Patrimonine, 2021, p. 2).

Addressing this challenge requires a shift in societal values and priorities, promoting responsible spending habits, and investing in essential services that benefit the broader population. Encouraging financial literacy and promoting alternative forms of celebration that are more sustainable and inclusive can also contribute to building a more equitable and prosperous society.

There is evidence that many women were against the Grande marriages and burned veils. In a YouTube video called *"Ali Soilihi and education of girls,"* many are receptive to the liberation constructed against the Grande Marriages (Umma Juzur lkamar, 2011).

The Shiromani—the red and white cloth used as a privacy veil by women—was collected and burned in an effort to destroy the vestiges of male supremacy and patriarchy (Ottenheimer, M. & Ottenheimer, H., 1985). The author tries in his demonstration to pass off a demonstration of women against the veil, for a demonstration in favor of the veil.

Revolution participant Said Hassane Jaffar writes that "I remember the great demonstration of the Comorian women against their liberation. They marched through the streets of Moroni: shouting their indignation, proud in the black habit that was said to be their prison" (Said Hassane Jaffar, 2003, paragraph 6).

The demonstration was created en masse by Ali Soilihi and supporters after the segment on Comorian women was broadcasted. Said Hassane Jaffar continues to say that "women and especially the many young girls, some of whom put on the veil for the first time, did so only to then take it off in the main square and burn it in front of a crowd of dumbfounded men" (Said Hassane Jaffar, 2003, paragraph 6)

Both religion and gender identity reached a chasm regarding both the veils and Grande marriages, the reaction was both ambiguous but supportive to ambivalent of the liberation to say the least. Navigating the intersection of religion, gender identity, and cultural practices can be highly nuanced and emotionally charged.

Defending the Revolution

"The significance of this day is that, whenever a country wrests its independence in a revolutionary way, [this independence] is not based on traditional and customary foundations" - Ali Soilihi to the Moissy on February 2, 1976, in Vwadju, Ngazidja (Great Island of the Comoros cited Lafon, 1995, pp. 28-29

Ali Soilihi designated reactionaries and class enemies of the revolution, to be fought within the framework of the "anti-feudal struggle," as "charlatans" (Giachino, 2005c). As Lenin paraphrased, the revolution is worth it, unless it can defend itself. This is congruent with Marx writing that "[v]iolence is the midwife of every old society pregnant with a new one" (Marx, 1867, p. 45).

Especially, violence was how the Comorian revolution was created into existence, breaking apart centuries of French rule. Another example of this violence is written by Fanon (1967), writing that "colonized subject discovers reality and transforms it through his praxis, his deployment of violence and his agenda for liberation. To the reactionaries, white washers of Comorian revolution, to the stomach for revolution" (p. xxxxv).

Against internal enemies and international capital such as France, the young socialist state had to defend the revolution. Fanon continues to write on the defending of the revolution:

> "Colonized subject is constantly on his guard: Confused by the myriad signs of the colonial world he never knows whether he is out of line. Confronted with a world configured by the colonizer, the colonized subject is always presumed guilty. The colonized does not accept his guilt, but rather considers it a kind of curse, a sword of Damocles. But deep down the colonized subject acknowledges no authority. He is dominated but not domesticated. He is made to feel inferior, but by no means convinced of his inferiority. He patiently waits for the colonist to let his guard down and then jumps on him. The muscles of the colonized are always tensed. It is not that he is anxious or terrorized, but he is always ready to change his role as game for that of hunter. The colonized subject is a persecuted man who is forever dreaming of becoming the persecutor. The symbols of society such as the police force, bugle calls in the barracks, military parades, and the flag flying aloft, serve not only as inhibitors but also as stimulants. They do not signify: 'Stay where you are.' But rather 'Get ready to do

> the right thing.' And in fact, if ever the colonized subject begins to doze off or forget, the colonist's arrogance and preoccupation with testing the solidity of the colonial system will remind him on so many occasions that the great showdown cannot be postponed indefinitely. This impulse to take the colonist's place maintains a constant muscular tonus. It is a known fact that under certain emotional circumstances an obstacle actually escalates action" (Fanon, 1967, xxxvii).

The colonized subject is depicted as navigating a world dominated by the colonizer's institutions and symbols, constantly unsure of their own position and legitimacy within it. Despite being subjected to feelings of guilt and inferiority imposed by the colonizer, they refuse to accept these as inherent truths and instead view them as oppressive burdens.

Lenin, Marx, and Fanon were key thinkers in both defending a revolution and defending a recently national oppressed people's revolution. We have only a couple of snippets of Comorians revolutionaries on how they grafted Lenin, Marx, Fanon, and Mao to their own traditions and needs. According to Comorian revolutionary activist at the time, Dini Nassur "repression was a necessary evil. You can't control the revolution. To transform society, it had to be shaken up (Giachino,2005c, para76)." But as to the contrary to another Comorian activist, Mohamed Dossar: "[t]here was a lot of unnecessary violence, which was not related to what we asked people. It had perverse effects: it brought people against us who should have been on our side. We made too many enemies at the same time. (Giachino,2005c, para 76)."

The small archipelago African socialist state of Comoros, completely on its own for the most part makes it different as Fanon suggests to" do the right thing "when it comes to revolutionary suppression of opponents.

Ali Soilihi was dealing with colonized Comorians' trauma and the coping mechanism of psycho-affective violence from centuries of Francophonia. Fanon (1967) describes this trauma from colonialism to: "not seeking to be perceived as a sweet, kind-hearted other who protects her child from a hostile environment, but rather a mother who constantly prevents her basically perverse child from committing suicide or giving free rein to its malevolent instincts. The colonial mother is protecting the child from itself, from its ego, its physiology, its biology, and its ontological misfortune (xxv)."

The metaphor of the colonial mother and her troubled child serves to illuminate the power dynamics inherent in colonial relationships, emphasizing the oppressive and controlling nature of colonial rule. It challenges romanticized notions of colonial benevolence and highlights the need to recognize and confront the injustices perpetuated by colonialism.

Sartre (1976) writes in the preface of Fanon on this trauma and repressive rage that explodes from a recently independent revolutionary state:

> "This repressed rage, never managing to explode, goes round in circles and wreaks havoc on the oppressed themselves. In order to rid themselves of it they end up massacring each other, tribes battle one against the other since they cannot confront

the real enemy-and you can count on colonial policy to fuel rivalries; the brother raising his knife against his brother believes he is destroying once and for all the hated image of their common debasement. But these expiatory victims do not satisfy their thirst for blood, and the only way to stop themselves from marching against the machine guns is to become our accomplices: the very dehumanization process they are rejecting will be speeded up by their own initiative. Under the amused gaze of the colonists, they protect themselves with supernatural safeguards, sometimes reviving awesome old myths, at other times tying themselves to meticulous rituals. The colonized, therefore, in his obsession, shuns his deep desires by inflicting on himself odd rites that monopolize him at every moment. They dance, that keeps them occupied; it relaxes their painfully contracted muscles, and what's more, the dance secretly mimes, often unbeknownst to them, they dare not voice, the murders they dare not commit. In some regions they use the last resort: possession (Satre,1967, p. lii)."

This passage delves into the psychological and social effects of colonial oppression on the colonized, depicting how repressed rage and frustration manifest in destructive ways within oppressed communities. The inability of the oppressed to direct their anger towards the real source of their suffering—the colonial oppressor—leads to internal strife and violence among themselves. Colonial policies exacerbate existing rivalries among tribes, fostering a cycle of conflict and bloodshed. The oppressed, unable to confront their true enemy, turn on each other, believing that by doing so, they are somehow eradicating the common debasement they endure.

However, these acts of violence do not assuage their thirst for justice. Instead, they become unwitting accomplices in their own dehumanization, furthering the colonial project by internalizing and perpetuating its destructive ideologies. To cope with their anguish and frustration, the colonized resort to various rituals and supernatural beliefs. These rituals serve as a distraction, offering temporary relief from their suffering. Yet, beneath the surface, these rituals also serve as a form of symbolic resistance, allowing the colonized to express their suppressed desires and emotions in a covert manner.

What became the contest-conflict of destroying the feudal-colonial past and as Fanon describes 'The colonized, underdeveloped man is a political creature in the most global sense of the term (vii)." That the defense of revolutionary violence as to: "wretch capitalist-feudalism norms, property, is the chaos, the disintegration of colonial law and order and stability a what Lange and other white travel writers and journals These write on the side of the colonialist, their legacy on the backs of exotic romantic and brute savage third world countries that write off the native to be a "a corrosive element…distorting everything which involved aesthetics or morals….an unconscious and incurable instrument of blind forces (Fanon,1967,xxv)."

This passage criticizes the norms and values perpetuated by capitalist-feudalism, portraying them as destructive forces that undermine colonial law, order, and stability. It also condemns the writings of white travel writers and journals who romanticize colonialism at the expense of the native population. The phrase "wretch capitalist-feudalism norms, property, is the chaos, the disintegration of colonial law and order and stability" suggests that the imposition of capitalist and feudal norms leads to disorder and instability within colonial societies. These norms are portrayed as oppressive and corrosive, disrupting traditional systems of governance and social cohesion. Yet the revolution needed to be defended. The way to defend the revolution physically was the Moissy.

Moissy, and the Republic of the Young People

"The world is yours, as well as ours, but in the last analysis, it is yours. Your young people, full of vigor and vitality, are in the bloom of life, like the sun at eight or nine in the morning. Our hope is placed on you………The world belongs to you. (Mao, 1961 p. 288)."

"He (Author's note: Soilihi) took the youth out of their hole and opened their minds to development-- Comorian revolutionary (Cited in Kweli,2024)."

Being only in his early 40's, Ali Soilihi conjured the revolution as a break with the past even when it came to age as a vanguard *tour d'force*. This is what became into being as the Moissy. This represented a Red Guard-esque graft that was influenced by Maoism and the Great Proletarian Cultural Revolution as the need to have the revolution be spread by the youth. The Red Guards in China were seen as the revolutionary *creme a la creme and* the impact on Global South Maoist-inspired revolutions. Unlike Maoist-inspired strategy in Comoros, there was no vanguard communist party leading the way. The Moissy was the primary physical defense of the revolution against conservative and charlatan elements.

After lowering the voting age to 14, a 'referendum' happened to approve a newly drafted constitution. Of the sixteen members of the National Popular Committee, all were in their last year of secondary school (Mattoir, 2004). A diplomat from the Federal Republic of Germany went to Moroni to discuss a grant for Comoros and went to the Ministry of Foreign Affairs. There he met the 17-year-old Comorian Minster of Foreign Affairs. Without even acknowledging the minister, the West German diplomat flew back to West Germany (Lamb, 1982).

The encounter between the West German diplomat and the 17-year-old Comorian Minister of Foreign Affairs underscores the diplomatic challenges posed by such unconventional political arrangements. The diplomat's failure to acknowledge the young minister may reflect a lack of awareness or understanding of Comoros' unique political context. Alternatively, it could indicate a disregard for the legitimacy of a government led by individuals perceived as inexperienced or unqualified due to their age. Regardless of the diplomat's intentions, the incident highlights the need for greater awareness and sensitivity to the diverse political landscapes and governance structures of different countries. It also underscores the importance of diplomatic engagement that respects the sovereignty and legitimacy of all nations, regardless of their internal political dynamics.

Wolin (2018) stated in the May 1968 revolution in France how students were primarily the force behind the cultural, anti-establishment, anti-de Gaullist response to French imperialism. We know that Soilihi was in Paris and was influenced by the May 1968 events in France. Here is where he possibly had contact with Maoism, influenced by the Cultural Revolution, the tenets of Global South revolution, and the reliance on the peasants as vanguards where the proletariat is not developed in Western capitalist countries. It is without a doubt the Moissy were based on the

Red Guards but with a very Islamic inspiration (see Comoros, ch. 6). One can surmise with contact and inspiration from the French and their inspiration of the Red Guard, the Moissy was created in an instance of *sui generis* because of the elder-feudal-sultan relations of power in Comoros. Like many liberation movements in the Global South, Soilihi, and the Comorian masses were influenced by Chinese communism of the 1960's:

> "The intrinsically anti-Eurocentric character of the Chinese Revolution can be understood according to the following three aspects. Firstly, it was a non-European society taking the initiative in making a revolution of historic importance; thus, the revolution proved, exactly as Lenin had predicted, that the Centre of creativity was outside the 'developed' areas. Secondly, Chinese theory and practice had revealed the enormous revolutionary strength of the peasantry, the basic force in the third World that was reviled and marginalized in Eurocentric thought...Thirdly, the Chinese Revolution is living proof of the deep historic roots of the progressive movement in the Third World, drawing upon both its pre-colonial roots.... and the tradition of national resistance.... (Biel, 2015, p. 149)."

The Chinese Revolution stands as a testament to the vitality and significance of anti-Eurocentric movements in the Global South. It challenges Eurocentric perspectives by demonstrating the agency and creativity of non-European societies in shaping their own destinies through revolutionary struggles. Regarding young people as the vanguard of revolution, a more apropos Mao (1969) writes:

> "The young people are the most active and vital force in society. They are the most eager to learn and the least conservative in their thinking. This is especially so in the era of socialism. We hope that the local Party organizations in various places will help and work with the Youth League organizations and go into the question of bringing into full play the energy of our youth. The Party organizations should not treat them in the same way as everybody else and ignore their special characteristics. Of course, the young people should learn from the old and other adults and should strive as much as possible to engage in all sorts of useful activities with their agreement (Mao,1961, p.290)."

While Mao emphasizes the importance of youth empowerment, he also advocates for mutual respect and cooperation between different age groups. He suggests that young people should learn from the experience and wisdom of older generations while also actively contributing to society through various meaningful activities.

Like the May 1968 revolt, French film director Jean-Luc Godard was inspired by Cultural Revolution of which the youth and Red Guard took active participation in the revolution. Cited in Wolin, Godard says in an interview:

"Youth, the moral and scientific quest, free from prejudices. One can't approve of all its forms…but this unprecedented cultural fact demands a minimum of attention, respect, and friendship (Wolin,2018, p. 115)."

Especially noting is the glaring fact of the reason that revolutionary youth would be the most important by Mao because a "sheet of blank paper carries no burden. The most beautiful characters can be written on it, the most beautiful pictures painted (Mao,1961, p34)." What became because of Maoist and Red Guards influence was the internal and external defender of the Comorian revolution, the Moissy being that blank sheet of paper.

Another ex-Moissy member Dini Nassur explains change of how politics were centered on the Moissy and how: "[b]efore, politics was the business of adults. Fighting for the population to know a better fate was an adventure for us. Trained – and indoctrinated – regularly, sometimes consulted, the "beardless" felt taken seriously. `We learned the basics for a week and then we went to the villages (*Mouvement Comorien des Jeunes Soilihistes*, 2017, post 5)

Despite their youth and relative inexperience, young people like Nassur were entrusted with responsibility and treated as meaningful contributors to the revolutionary project. This recognition instilled both confidence and a sense of purpose, transforming their involvement into more than mere political duty, it became an adventure charged with the optimism of shaping a better collective future. In this way, the revolution was experienced not only as a struggle for structural change, but also as a formative process through which a generation discovered its political agency and imagined new possibilities for the fate of the population.

After going to the Mouridya villages, the Mossy as per Dini Nassur continues that "[a]fterwards, we came to report. Soilihi was welcoming us all to the presidential palace. (*Mouvement Comorien des Jeunes Soilihistes,* 2017, post 5)." The Moissy gave agency to many disaffected teenagers to take part in politics in all spheres from being directors of government and an internal defender of the revolution on-the-ground.

Denard was in the archipelago when Soilihi started organizing the Moissy. His testimony gives great insight to Soilihi being inspired by the Red Guards. From Denard's memoirs there is the reason for Moissy as per Ali Soilihil "[t]he country, needs a people's militia… They will also have to be breeders and peasants in order to participate fully in the life of the people. I want a Chinese- style army! In order to set it up. I will immediately disband the police and the prison administration. (Denard, para 60)."

This quote is the epitome of the connection between the Red Guard and the Moissy. Further evidence regarding the lumpenproletarian status of the Moissy, the charismatic, the popular style of Soilihi comes from ex-revolutionary veteran Ma Elaniou:

> "Never had he (Ali Soilih – Editor's note) been so relaxed, nor so eloquent. Reuniting with his comrades, with the emotion that you can imagine parricides, assassins, brigands, thieves of all kinds, and of course crooks, he was never so happy. And never were the hundred crooks so proud: just think! One of them had succeeded practically alone, what they all dreamed of: putting honest people in a box. No virtue,

> no article of law, no morality had citizenship. They were radiant convicts! They saw in the exceptional success of one of their comrades (Ali Soilihi – Editor's note), the justification of their life, they could finally raise the flag the color of blood (Said Hassane Jaffar, 2003, para 23)."

The description of them as "radiant convicts" means that the lumpenproletariat was represented as a class in liberation and empowerment in their newfound identity as accomplices to a successful scheme. Their success is seen as a rebellion against conventional morality and law, symbolized by their ability to "raise the flag the color of blood." There has always been a precedent of both anarchist and Maoist tendencies of arming the lumpenproletariat, the criminals, and unemployed as the true oppressed within the Global South. In Comorian circumstance, the Moissy as per Said Hassane Jaffar, makes sure that the lumpenproletariat, is the vanguard of the Moissy.

Soilihi believed that adults were not up to the task of vanguardist revolution. The uplifting of youth as a vanguardist subject for the revolution was because of the strife of elders and youth. Shikomori-speaking Comorians (wageni) was the primarily elder and conservative generations and younger Zanzibar-born or Malagasy Comorians (wazalia). The conservative Wageni represented the rule of sultan-feudalism, the regimes of Abdullahism, and Jaffarism and the need to break free from these regimes.

Ex-President of the Comorian Assembly, Said Oiffir left school in his final year to engage in the revolution. *The Movement Comorienne des Jeunes Socialistes* (The Movement of Young Comorian Soilihists), writes Soilihi "did not reject the generation of adults, but they had reason to have reservations. They couldn't fully play the revolutionary game. They had families to feed... We kind of agreed to sacrifice ourselves, 24 hours a day (Giachino,2005c, para 10)." Hence, the Moissy were the vanguardist entity that carried out defense of the "revolutionary game." Continuing, Said Oiffir of the *Mouvement Comorien des Jeunes Soilihstes* wrote that Soilihi "planned actions that allowed young people to be on the ground and show that they were useful for something (Giachino,2005c, para 10)." In contrary to the conservative elite being aligned and equated with maturity, Soilihi wanted to continue the clear break from reaction and French imperialism by having the youth and oppressed as members of the Moissy: "Soilih had aroused vocations of technicians and, as the Comoros lacked them, the children of the revolution were finally able to integrate into the country. With success: we find them at the technical controls of the country... but also in many supporting political roles (Comoroes-Online.com, no year, para 45)."

As a result of Soilih's initiatives, the children of the revolution were able to integrate into various sectors of the country, notably occupying technical positions critical for the nation's development and functioning. This success is shown by their presence at the technical controls of the country, where their expertise and skills contribute to its progress and stability.

In an interview with Latimer Rangers and French Radio International with Ali Soilihi on 1 February 1976, Soilihi gives great insight on the raison *d'etre* of socialist policy about the Moissy, and international socialist advisors and instructors. Soilihi discusses the enthusiasm of the youth and the policy of the armed peasant, literacy programs, and needed liberation of Maore/Mayotte:

"We did so first of all to give them military training so that they would be able to defend their country, but this was also done with a view to the Mayotte affair. I must, however, tell you that the young people who are currently in the military quite apart from this Mayotte affair which we consider an aberration are destined to get very strong political training because these are militants who fought for years against the regime in power against colonial status. These are mostly political militants. We are thus pushing their political training so as to open the doors for them to a worldwide international policy. We are going to start them into the principles of literacy because many of them have not had a chance to go to school and we are going to initiate them into the principles of calculation arithmetic. We are also going to teach them a certain number of development techniques in agriculture technology and construction because the normal vocation of these young people excludes the accident of Mayotte. These young people must be with the rest of the nation everywhere in the villages in order to bring to the inhabitants a spirit of renewal not with a lot of words but by getting down to work by working with them in the fields by helping them build the warehouses for the cooperatives cantonal

> offices and obviously also by helping them in the fields. This is the principle of the hoe and the rifle." (Authors emp) (Rangers, 1976, page. 3). "

The importance of political education for these young militants, many of whom had been involved in fighting against the earlier regime. The authorities looked to equip them with the skills and knowledge necessary to participate actively in national and international politics. The principle of "the hoe and the rifle" encapsulates the ideology of combining agricultural work with military preparedness, emphasizing both productive labor and defense readiness as integral to the nation's progress and security.

Critics from the Western left might attack Moissy and the revolutionary vanguard as ultra-left heretics. But the realization is that Soilihi and the Comorian oppressed was socialized and forced by real reasons to break away historical oppressor agents, by the creation of the Moissy. Mao (1961) stipulates what judgement means about someone is revolutionary or not:

> "How should we judge whether a youth is a revolutionary? How can we tell? There can only be one criterion, namely, whether or not he is willing to integrate himself with the broad masses of workers and peasants and does so in practice. If he is willing to do so and actually does so, he is a revolutionary; otherwise, he is a nonrevolutionary or a counter revolutionary. If today he integrates himself with the masses of workers and

> peasants, then today he is a revolutionary, if tomorrow he ceases to do so (p.56)."

The emphasis on practical engagement underscores the importance of direct involvement in the real-life struggles of ordinary people. It suggests that revolutionary commitment is proved through tangible acts of solidarity, mobilization, and collective action aimed at challenging oppressive systems and advocating for the interests of the marginalized and oppressed.

YouTube played a key part in giving me audible and visible insight to the revolution in clips, English documentaries, and UN reports. Two examples are from YouTube, and another is from a UN report.

One on the page titled *Ali Soilihi Mtsachiwa _ la révolution comorienne de 1975*, published by Bambao-RTV Mvouni-Bambao (2015), presents scenes presumably showing the drilling of Moissy with wooden rifles, in French uniform-like caps, and Young Pioneer style uniforms (Appendix C, Fig. 5).

Another reference is from a UN report that the Moissy wore red shirts and red scarves to match their revolutionary vigor (Official Documents, 1979. United States: UN).

These examples underscore the importance of platforms like YouTube in issuing information and documenting historical events, offering a multimedia perspective that combines audiovisual elements with textual sources such as UN reports. This allows for a more comprehensive understanding of the revolution and its visual representations.

Soilihism and Internationalism

International policy as per the Social and Secular Republic was clear cut following to break off France as the first international enemy while having some international allies to support the Comorian revolution. Ali Soilihi is the only Comorian leader who appointed France as "enemy number one". The same, who, in *Le Monde* of December 4, 1975, declared:

"[we] note that these French authorities who managed to make us give in (…) will now try to break our economy, our administration, by brutally cutting technical aid and abruptly withdrawing all resources from us (Giachino,2005a, para 6)."

This statement seems to convey a sentiment of resistance against perceived external pressure, possibly from French authorities, and the fear of economic and administrative repercussions. It suggests a belief that these capitalist authorities are employing tactics to weaken or undermine the economy and administrative structure of the speaker's entity. The use of phrases like "make us give in" and "try to break our economy" indicates a sense of coercion and vulnerability. Overall, it reflects a stance of defiance and concern about the potential consequences of external actions.

As for Soilihi's statement, "We need France," it could be interpreted in various ways. Politicians, especially in developing or smaller countries, often must balance international relations, and such a statement might reflect a strategic diplomatic move. If Soilihi is in the process of political evolution, it might be an example of a pragmatic or diplomatic approach, rather than an indication of dependency. The Marxist Internet Archive might be presenting an analysis of Comoros in a certain ideological context, but it could also be an outlier among other possible readings of the situation.

> "Clearly neo-colonialism is the main danger in Afrika, as new Head of State Ahmed Abdallah, who took militant & uncompromising stand against French. imperialism's control of his newly independent nation, was overthrown only 30 days after they declared · independence. Ali Soilih's first statement after the coup he led, betrayed the whole plot - "We need France ... "But in reality, France was exploiting the natural resources of the Comoro Island s; France needs the Comoro Island s for super profits and has overthrown the new government thru native agents. The Comoro Islands are the world's second largest producer of vanilla, & exports essence of perfume (supplying 70% of France's production), coconut fiber, sisal, cocoa, clove, coffee, pepper, wood & lava for construction (marxistinternetarchive.com)."

The statement attributed to Ali Soilih, acknowledging the need for France despite its exploitative practices, reflects the complex realities faced by post-colonial nations. While recognizing the importance of diplomatic relations and economic ties, it also suggests the inherent power imbalances and dependencies that often characterize relationships between former colonies and their former colonizers.

It's interesting that only two international socialist publications have given print space to the Comoros, specifically *Unity and Struggle* in 1975 and the Communist Party of France (Marxist-Leninism). This reflects the generally limited international attention given to smaller states like the Comoros, especially during a time when larger geopolitical issues and the Cold War were dominating global discourse.

These outlets, with their Marxist-Leninist ideologies, would have seen the Comoros as a part of the global struggle for anti-imperialist independence and sovereignty, especially as the country gained independence from France in 1975.

The Left Communist group *Unity and Struggle* had in its print headline: "Neo-Colonialism Subverts Independence in Comoro Islands," but with probably limited information, the paper erroneously supports the bourgeois nationalist Abdallah against Soilihi. Whether *Unity and Struggle* had different politics about Comoros, the Global South, and Maoism is ambiguous. Either they misquote, or there is insight unbeknownst to the literature.

The idea of international socialist countries supporting Comoros in terms of solidarity, education, and assistance is intriguing, especially when considering the broader historical context. In the immediate aftermath of Comoros' independence from France in 1975, the country was navigating the complex terrain of post-colonial state-building, and socialist nations with an anti-imperialist stance were often seen as allies by newly independent states in Africa, Asia, and Latin America.

Roinka (2020) writes that diplomatically, Senegal represented Comorian interests around the world. Informational sources are limited and found only in People's Republic of China, Tanzania, DPRK, and Seychelles. Roinka (2020) writes that diplomatically, Senegal represented Comorian interests around the world. Informational sources are limited and found only in People's Republic of China, Tanzania, DPRK, and Seychelles.

People's Republic of China

International support and assistance came from chiefly People's Republic of China, DPRK, and Tanzania. Because of influence of Red Guards, Maoism, and the Cultural Revolution, there is no doubt that international recognition and support chiefly came from People's Republic of China. Comoros sent nine students to study in China (Bakar,1988). In an issue of the *Peking Review* in 1976, a message from Soilihi to Chairman Hua Kuo-feng on October 31st states:

> "Warm congratulations on your election as Chairman of the Central Committee of the Communist Party of China and Chairman of the Military Commission. We are convinced that under your leadership the revolutionary policy of Mao Tseung will win still more successes, and we wish that the friendly relations with your country will be further strengthened (Marxists.org)."

Soilihi expresses confidence in the recipient's leadership, believing that under their guidance, the revolutionary policy of Mao Zedong will achieve further successes. Additionally, the Soilihi expresses a desire for friendly relations between their respective countries to be strengthened.

Ali Mohamed dit Niza's letter to the Peking Review and the subsequent publication of an article titled

Dietsche

"Population Growth" is a fascinating piece of historical correspondence, especially considering the context of the Cold War and the broader ideological movements during the 1970s:

> "I've recently read the article 'Developmental Trends in Chinese Population Growth" which appeared in Beijing Review issue No. 2. The population issue is of international concern. Due to the uncontrolled baby boom, this important and urgent problem cannot be solved until the year 2000. This is one of the factors hindering development in Africa, Latin America, and Asia. I'm delighted to see that China is the first country to give its due consideration to this matter (Ali Mohamed dit Niza,1976, para 23)."

This example highlights an international connection between a Comorian revolutionary and the People's Republic of China, underscoring the transnational dimensions of revolutionary struggle in the postcolonial era.

It further demonstrates a profound revolutionary consciousness attentive not only to questions of national liberation and sovereignty but also to broader concerns such as population growth, which was increasingly framed as both a developmental challenge and a political issue within global socialist discourse.

In an issue of the *Peking Review* of June 11, 1976, an article titled *"Comoros Government Delegation"* Salim Himidi,

Minister of Internal Affairs meets with Vice-Premier Chang Chun-chia. There was a banquet in honor of the delegation telling the Comoros delegation that the PRC supported Comoros for its stand against imperialism. As per the article both delegations exchanged certainties of support of cooperation.

Salim Himidi said that the PRC and Comoros "knew the same sufferings in the past and are today still confronted with the same precautions on the part of the enemies of progress and emancipation of the people" (*Peking Review*, 1976).

Himidi also discussed how both feudalistic capitalisms has been discussed as the parallelism of both China and Comoros having a part occupied by imperialist forces. As per the article there was not any mention of aid of continuing the struggle of Maoism. The article and the meeting said more of a meeting to start cooperation talks (marxistinternetarchive.com).

Salim Himidi emphasized the shared history of suffering and ongoing challenges faced by both China and Comoros in their struggles against imperialism and for the progress and emancipation of their people. He drew parallels between the feudalistic capitalisms present in both countries and highlighted the common struggle against imperialist forces.

Seychelles

The only mention of a solidarity aid package between Comoros and another African country was Seychelles. Roinak (2020) makes the claim that Comoros in act of solidarity describes Comorian socialism to have it had enough surplus in aid that the "the Comorian state also provided substantial aid in the military and education fields to the Seychelles archipelago which had just gained independence in 1976. (Roinak,2020, para 5)." This act of solidarity implies that Comoros, despite facing its own challenges and being a relatively small nation, was willing to support and aid another newly independent country in its efforts to establish itself and develop. The provision of aid in military and education fields shows a commitment to fostering stability, security, and human capital development in the Seychelles.

Democratic People's Republic of Korea

North Korea Quarterly (1977) presents that the DPRK relationships were connected upon Comoros break from France in its bourgeois revolution. DPRK established an embassy and on 18 January 1977, ambassador So Jinyong met Vice President Mohamed Hassan and Soilihi. Again, history has lost what kind of aid, or anything was given or exchanged between the two countries. As per *North Korean Quarterly* dated on March 15, 1978, ambassador presented a gift from Kim Ill Sung to Comoros which said "full support and firm solidarity with the Korean people's struggle" to achieve an independent and peaceful Korean reunification (*North Korea Quarterly*,1977, p. 3)."

There are no further details indicating whether students, technicians, material aid, or military assistance were provided by the DPRK to support the Comorian revolutionary cause. Even if some form of assistance was extended, it appears to have been limited in scope and ultimately ineffective in mitigating the external isolation that characterized Comoros' position during this period. This lack of meaningful support underscores the difficulties faced by small revolutionary movements in the global periphery, which often sought solidarity from socialist states yet remained marginal within the broader strategic priorities of Cold War geopolitics. While the DPRK projected itself as a staunch ally of anti-imperialist struggles, its engagement with Comoros—unlike with certain liberation movements in Africa and Asia—seems to have been symbolic rather than transformative, leaving the Comorian revolutionaries without the external leverage needed to counterbalance their isolation on the international stage.

The defense of the revolution, the organization of daily life, and the dissemination of propaganda to mobilize the masses could only extend so far in sustaining a fragile socialist state. What could not be anticipated were the 'triple troubles' that soon followed: a volcanic eruption and two massacres that compounded the challenges of governance. Confronted with these crises, the young socialist archipelago was forced to respond with limited resources and under precarious international circumstances, revealing both the resilience and the vulnerability inherent in revolutionary state-building during its formative years.

Triple Trouble: Madagascar Massacres, Mountain Explosions, and Iconi

Majunga Rataka

Three calamities that would stretch the socialist state's resources to the maximum would be the Karthala explosion, Majuna Rataka, and Iconi massacres. Ex-patriot Comorians living in Madagascar, like Ali Soilihi, experienced a tragic rupture between the local Madagascar citizens.

Combination of economic policies and the government's 'Malgachisation' politics created a Malagasy migration. This created a racist attack on Madagascar's Comorian populace. Anti-Comorian Malagasy reactionary culture created policies of xenophobia of Comorian migrants as either non-African or as so-called the "Arab bloodsuckers" (Roberts, 2021).

Such attitudes and policies contribute to social tensions and discrimination against the Comorian community in Madagascar, creating a hostile environment for migrants and exacerbating divisions within society. This underscores the importance of addressing underlying systemic issues of racism and discrimination to promote inclusivity, tolerance, and social cohesion within diverse communities.

In the district of Fifio in the city of Mahajanga on December 19, 1976, a Betsirebaka child defecated in the area of a Comorian family. A member of the Comorian family, in exasperation, smearing the child with his own feces. In the community of Betsirebakans, this violated many taboos. To make amends the Comorian community gave a zebu and some money. But the Betsirebkan family refused any offering (Roberts, 2021).

A survivor of the Rataka massacre, known as 'Gorille,' a 26-year-old Comorian from Mahajanga in 1976, later recounted the events that unfolded in its aftermath. His testimony provides a rare first-hand perspective of violence, offering insight not only into the immediate human toll but also into the atmosphere of fear, uncertainty, and resilience that shaped the lived experience of the revolution's participants.

"Initially, it was an altercation between a Grand Comorian and a Betsirebaka in Fifio, near Mandzarsoa. At the time, it was a small neighborhood, a small football field. Concordant versions attest to the immediate cause of the drama. A Betsirebaka child makes his excrement twice in the courtyard of a Comorian family. Exasperated, a member of it smears the child with his excrement. Today is December 19. "We don't play with feces. No one would like it (Saindou.2021, para 7)."

The next day, the Rataka in the Mahabibo district erupted for three days. The Betsirebaka resorted to machetes , mutilations, and rape of Comorians. Betsirebaka burned and looted houses of local districts (Rijke-Epstein, 2017.) During the Rataka, it is estimated around 1,000 to 2,000 Comorians were killed in violence against them. The alleged "criminal" scapegoat was arrested and when the Betsirebaka went to the police station, the mob of Betsirerbaka attacked the Mahabibo mosque.

Regarding the attack on the mosque, says Gorille:

> "[t]he Betsirebaka threw stones inside the mosque, the Comorians present responded, there were two deaths," The Comorians organized patrols to protect their neighborhoods including the Abattori. Reaction is taken seriously by the Comorian side, but not by the authorities. Curious Mahajanga police open fire on Comorians. During this the Betsirebaka planned on occupying to companies and other neighborhoods worked by Comorians (Saindou,2021, para 5)."

    This act constituted a deliberate effort to target and intimidate the Comorian population, functioning not only as an episode of violence but also as a calculated strategy of political repression. By instilling fear among the broader populace, such actions sought to undermine popular support for the revolutionary project and to reinforce patterns of control through coercion.

    Because of the Malagasy government response to the Rataka, the Comorian government decided upon an air lift to liberate fellow Comorians. At least 15,000 Comorians were migrated to the Comorian archipelago on Belgium's Air *Sabena* planes. From this survivor of the riot were called "Sabenas."

There is many suspects of the reason why the massacre took place, why it perpetuated to such heights. One such reason is how many Comorians today believe that Ali Soilihi created the massacre to get more Comorians back to the archipelago. Yet there is some doubt of whether Ali Soilihi's management as well as if Soilihi is to blame for the incident. Said Hassane Jaffar discuss how Elanois dissuades fault about that Soilihi's attitude towards Rataka survivors:

> "Nothing, absolutely nothing, in all that. Ali Soilihi has done finds favor in the eyes of the author. Not even the congratulations of the Office of the United Nations High Commissioner for Refugees, addressed to the Comorian authorities, for having been able to assume alone, the management of all the problems, related to the repatriation and accommodation of all the Comorian survivors, victims of massacres in Majunga (Said Hassane Jaffar, 2003, paragraph 8)."

Even accomplishments such as managing the repatriation and accommodation of Comorian survivors of massacres in Majunga do not find favor in the author's eyes. This shows a deep-seated bias or disdain towards Ali Soilihi, where even positive achievements are dismissed or criticized.

But then-Minister of Foreign Affairs Mouzawar Abdallah, who also was part of the Comorian delegation, writes against this heresy saying, "[t]he day when this extent will be better identified, I assure you that those who blamed these massacres on Ali Soilihi, have committed a crime at the national level" (Saindou, 2021, para 19).

Contrary to this, Said Hassane Jaffar supports the hypothesis that the Rataka was plotted by Ali Soilihi to gain more financial support from the UN and possibly the OAU. Said Hassane Jaffar writes that "this, in passing, by inflicting a scathing denial to the assertions raised here or there, suggesting that the Ali Soilihi regime was hunting for subsidies" (Saindou, 2021, para 12).

This is the only statement at the time of writing regarding Soilihi using a racist and xenophobic incident as the Rataka for his own means. To this day, the Rataka still taints the Comorians and Madagascans with a cultural "blanket of silence" that prevents both communities from mourning and making peace and justice.

My unpublished poem "Sabenas to Soilihi-land" is to commiserate the victims of xenophobia and racism in the riots:

> "in the district of Fifio,
>
> In the city of Mahajana
>
> a Betsirebaka child…
>
> broke custom and sacriledged on the lawn---
>
> of a Comorian family
>
> ---response
>
> -----was
>
> Somewhat smeared the child
>
> Sacrilegiously back
>
> And---Rutaka

Dietsche

> Exploded
>
> In Mahbibo
>
> ---victims retreated
>
> In flying Sabenas
>
> To Soilihi-land"
>
> --- (Dietsche, unpublished poem).

Karthala

In contrast to the Majunga massacre, the eruption of Mount Karthala represents a blind spot in the historical record concerning how the Social and Secular Republic of the Comoros mobilized rescues and support for its citizens during a volcanic earthquake. The scarcity of information raises questions about the state's capacity to respond to ecological disaster within the framework of a fragile revolutionary government. Nevertheless, this episode offers a potentially valuable case study for examining how the resources of a centrally planned economy were—or were not—mobilized to meet the challenges posed by natural catastrophes in socialist contexts. Comparisons might be drawn with better-documented examples such as the management of the Chernobyl disaster in Ukraine,

recurring flood relief efforts in the Democratic People's Republic of Korea, or Cuba's extensive hurricane preparedness and recovery systems, each of which illustrates the complex interplay between socialist state structures, resource allocation, and ecological vulnerability.

Dietsche

The volcanic crater of Karthala overlooks the capital of Moroni. Karthala is an active volcano and the highest point of the Comoros at 2,361 m (7,746 ft) above sea level. It is the southernmost and larger of the two shield volcanoes forming the largest island in the nation of Comoros. The Karthala volcano is continually active, having erupted more than twenty times since the 19th century. Frequent eruptions have shaped the volcano's 3 km by 4 km summit caldera, but the island has largely escaped broad destruction. Yet in 1977, the volcano exploded, and we can assume that this was a major strain on the central economy and major rearranging of priorities for Soilihi. **The unpublished poem** "it's huge, Karthala!!!!" is dedicated to the survivors of the volcano:

"Speak volumes Karthala

cauldron caldera seawater amongst

coral outlier

islands of moon geography

star moon paper plate moon

opposite end of flashlight moon surround rice stars

eclipsing Indian sea sun

are clouds just a passing phrase

in tropicalized ocean

--- Dietsche (unpublished poem)."

Dietsche

Iconi

There has never been a real investigation into what happened at Iconi. There is however many documents and testimonial evidence of what transpired. As per powerbroker Lebret, the argument was over what seemed to be a betrayal over democratic centralist policies and decision making between the Mongozi and the Moissy. The Moissy was told to use blank bullets in the altercation with what was perceived as counterrevolutionary strife or ambiguous understanding. But from sources, there is no sign that the Moissey treated the quarrelers as counterrevolutionaries:

> "The residents were hostile to the new method. Because at the beginning, before making a decision, Ali invited a sample of people to the palace from whom he asked their opinion. There came a time when he changed his method. He saw that these people were a hindrance when he had to move quickly. So, Ikoni is no longer involved in the debate, the young people of the village committee are not helping things, the Revolution is advancing [getting tougher], we stop here, we punish there, therefore, the people of Ikoni have decided to react they locked the young people of the

Committee in the ngouwou. The army had to intervene. The commander of the general staff, Mohamed Ahmada, said to Ali: "There! We have to disembark at Ikoni because the Committee has been sequestered." Ali told them: "If you go to Ikoni, don't go there with live ammunition – I know the people of Ikoni. Go there with blank bullets, just to dissuade them... And first, we have to send the Mwassi there, they are young people and activists! And Ikoni, we cannot consider him an enemy of the regime, even if, from time to time, they show their dissatisfaction with the regime... You will try to discuss it with them. And if it doesn't work and you have to go for it yourself, go for it, but without live [bullets]." But Cdt X., the regional commander, said to himself: 'How? Am I going to go there, unarmed? I know the Ikoni, they are tough guys who will take us down. I'm not going to...' He doesn't say anything about it to Ali, he persists, he leaves with weapons [loaded with live ammunition]. And when they're there... At one point, I was called. I was in front of Al Maarouf hospital. My wife was there at the time. And I see ambulances arriving at full speed, with their audible alert... "What's happening?" So, they called me and Mohamed Ahmada, the Chief of Staff, said to me: "Call Ali, please, and tell him that in Ikoni, something happened..."

> They were afraid to call themselves. "But why don't you call him yourself?" Because Ali's number was only known to me and the Chief of Staff. Even though, to communicate with him, from abroad, I had to go to the post office to pick up the communication and pass it on to Ali. We shouldn't be able to contact him directly, at any time... In Ikoni, something happened... It seems that there were deaths. I am in front of the hospital. I see, it's true! There are a lot of people we take to the hospital." Ali said nothing for a long moment... "Ahamada, our diet is over!" When we start killing each other like that, it means that our effort is doomed to failure..." And it was true. It was March 1978 (Masawi, 2023, para 7)."

This passage describes a shift in Ali Soilihi's approach to governance and conflict resolution in Iconi. Initially, Ali Soilihi sought the opinions of a sample of people before making decisions. However, he eventually realized that this approach slowed down the decision-making process, leading him to exclude certain individuals from the debate and take tougher measures to enforce the revolution's agenda.

From the available accounts, it can be inferred that the people of Iconi reacted by detaining young members of the Committee, prompting the intervention of the army. Soilihi instructed the troops to proceed with caution, explicitly recommending against the use of live ammunition and emphasizing dialogue as the preferred course of action.

However, these directives were disregarded at the local level: a regional commander chose to intervene with live ammunition, thereby escalating the confrontation in direct contradiction to Soilihi's orders.

This portrays Ali Soilihi's attempt to balance firm leadership with a desire to avoid unnecessary violence and keep dialogue, highlighting the challenges and complexities of governance during this period. We do know that it was not Ali Soilihi's intention to shoot at fellow Comorians. Activist Takidine Salim recalls talking to Ali Soilihi on the day of the event:

> "I returned to the Comoros on the day of the Ikoni incidents. I went to see Ali; I found him crying in his office; he said to me: "You realize! These idiots! They went there. They killed Comorians. I don't admit it! This is important justice to be done to him. Ali did not know that the soldiers had left Vwadjou, with [real] weapons and cartridges, to subdue Ikoni. It was a dramatic affair which affected him a lot and which caused him to lose a lot of weight (Masawi, 2023, para 7)."

This portrayal adds depth to Ali Soilihi's character, revealing both his vulnerability and his humanity in the face of tragedy. It underscores the immense weight of leadership and the personal toll exacted by decisions made under crisis conditions.

As Mohamed Ahamada Tabibou explains, the roots of the disagreement lay in cultural tensions surrounding the vestiges of the Grand Mariage and the role of the Moissy. These long-standing institutions, central to Comorian social life, came into conflict with the revolutionary government's attempts to reform or curtail them, highlighting the friction between tradition and modernizing socialist policies.

The confrontation at Iconi thus cannot be understood merely as a political or military misstep, but also as an eruption of deeper cultural contestations over identity, authority, and the legitimacy of change.

"There was violence because the people around him were not well prepared. // There was violence. I remember that in Ikoni, there was a shooting at the mosque and several people died. I went to the funeral in Ikoni because I answered a call on the Radio asking for people to dig the graves. The soldiers shot at people who were at the mosque during morning prayers. It was around 5 a.m. We decreed the curfew because we did not want the Ikoni to demonstrate. There was a curfew, only for the people of Ikoni. The origin of this shooting? The Ikoni had put the young people of the Committee, responsible for applying Ali's directives, in a well. They contested a decision of this Committee which had imposed as a dowry, during the marriage of a girl from a large family, a chair... However, the father of this girl had planned to marry her, according to the procedure of Lavish Marriage. This shamed the family. So, the population reacted and locked the Committee in a well. There was a first ultimatum, given to the population of Ikoni to release the young people; they ignored it. That's when the Army intervened and there was this shooting. Some Ikoni broke curfew; they were arrested and marched from Ikoni to Mroni... (Masawi, 2023, para 7)."

The violence erupted following a dispute involving the young members of the Committee tasked with implementing Soilihi's directives. The conflict arose when the Committee imposed a dowry requirement during the marriage of a girl from a prominent family, a move that clashed with the Grande Marriage tradition planned by her father.

In response, members of the local population detained the Committee members in a well, a confrontation that escalated tragically. Eleven people lost their lives, a consequence of confusion over whether to arm the Moissy with live ammunition.

For some observers, this incident left a lasting stain on Ali Soilihi's reputation as a leader, highlighting the complex challenges of enforcing revolutionary policies in a society deeply rooted in traditional practices.

It remains uncertain whether French authorities were aware of the shooting. However, it is reasonable to assume that Lebret, who was involved in handling both previous coups, was present during the massacre. Likewise, it is plausible that information regarding the unfolding events and potential coup activity was transmitted to plotters based in Paris. This convergence of local violence, revolutionary policy, and international intrigue underscores the precarious position of Soilihi's government and the multifaceted pressures shaping Comorian politics during this turbulent period.

Returning From the Point of no Return

Three years of Soilihist socialism unfortunately did not disrupt centuries of exploitation and transform the Comorian masses. Like every other place that called itself socialist in the world, it is not conducive to say socialism failed in Comoros.

French sanctions, French imperialist support of Maore/Mayotte, lukewarm support by Tanzania and Madagascar, centuries of costly Grande Marriages, and sultan-conservatism, left Soilihi with a lot to overcome.

As per Keri (2019), Ali Soilihi called his socialism the "the point of no return." In pursuit of the "point of no return," Soilihi was launched in a race against time and against his enemies.

Many Comorians revolutionary activists say that time was not on Soilihi's side. Veteran revolutionary activist Youssouf Said says that " Ali Soilihi tackled too many things at the same time. It is normal that there have been dissatisfactions (Keri, 2019, para 34)". But there was a real acknowledgement by Ali Soilihi that even though he was sick himself. Ahamadi Boura writes that:

> "At the end, I told him that things were no longer going well, that people were

> unhappy... And that's how I noticed that he was seriously ill; because I happened to speak for an hour without being interrupted, while, usually and previously, he would have immediately responded to each of my sentences (Masawi,2023, para 8)."

Besides his documented cancer, Ali Solihi continued to want a need for the revolutionary pace to quicken to create and combine a healthy democratic institution in the mourdiyas, defend the revolution by the Moissy, make contact in solidarity with other popular revolutionary states, and to demolish visages of French imperialist rule.

Revolutionary activist-Youssouf Said writes that the state was unable to be fully functional and healthy to support and provide for the needs of the masses. Soilihi must have felt that France would possibly usurp him by Denard. Youssouf Said writes that "[b]ecause he (Authors Note: Soilihi) realized he was doomed, because he affected the interests of France. He wanted to pass on to others what he wanted to do (Giachino, 2005a.para 5)." Giachino(2005d) writes that Soilihi wanted to have other generations finish what he started:

> "Ali Soilih felt a real strength behind him. The strength of young people, of power, and that of the left-wing countries that supported it. It was necessary to take advantage of this so as not to give the reactionaries time to react. France was working for its downfall. He thought that if he managed to achieve things, to complete

> the Mourdiya, there would be self-defense on the part of the people. In the Seychelles, which applied the same administrative model as Ali Soilih and received his military aid, the mercenaries were pushed back by the population (Giachino,2005d, para 45)."

Soilihi believed it was crucial to capitalize on this strength to prevent reactionary forces from gaining momentum. Ali Soilihi saw France as working against him, but he believed that by carrying out significant projects like completing the mourdiya buildings, he could bolster the people's ability to defend themselves. He drew parallels with the Seychelles, where a similar administrative model was implemented, and military aid provided by Ali Soilihi helped repel mercenaries, proving the effectiveness of his approach.

To gauge support of himself and socialism, Comoros had a referendum on October 1977. Only 55 percent of the voters supported a new constitution proposed by his socialist government. Problems with the Moissy as well as problems with the centralized government are considered to be a constant reality. Attacks by the Moissy on real and imagined political opponents escalated, and raids on mosques were common, as well as refugees fleeing to Maore/Mayotte.

Severe food shortages in 1976–77 required the government to seek aid internationally and forced the young nation to divert its already limited export earnings from economic development to buys of rice and other staples. Mukonoweshuro writes that importing foodstuffs does not mean that the socialist project was going badly. This need policy only meant that "[i]mportation of basics is what a fundamental need, a right, and …of a socialist state" (Mukonoweshuro, 1990, p. 567).

Said Dhoiffir, President of the Assembly of the Union, who was the coordinator of the National People's Committee, writes on how dismal Soilihism was. He said that "[w]e knew that things were going badly" (Giachino, 2005a, para 5). Said Dhoiffir's perspective on the state of affairs under Ali Soilihi's leadership criticizes what he perceives as the shortcomings of Soilihi's socialist policies. He emphasizes the importance of importing basic necessities as a fundamental need and right in a socialist state. Dhoiffir's remarks suggest dissatisfaction with the economic conditions and policies implemented during the period of Soilihism, showing a sense of disillusionment with the regime's effectiveness

Dhoiffir continued his discussions with Soilihi, engaging in deliberations that reflected both political strategy and crisis management. Their exchanges shed light on the internal dynamics of the revolutionary leadership, revealing how decisions were negotiated amidst social tensions, security challenges, and the pressures of upholding socialist reforms in a culturally complex environment.

> "We talked about it from time to time to the president. He answered us that he was going to try to remedy it but that the commandos (*Author's Note*: commandos were the Moissy) were poorly educated, that they found themselves with responsibilities that fell from the sky, and that they had trouble finding a happy medium. And then, we had the impression that for him, it was part of the revolution. And we couldn't manage to control the base committees (Giachino, 2005a.para 5)."

This indicates that Soilihi was aware of certain tensions surrounding the Moissy, understanding that the challenges they posed were rooted more in education and social practice than in ideological opposition, like the dynamics evident in the Iconi incident.

The activist Abbas Jusuf reportedly informed Soilihi of his opposition to the Moissy serving as the armed enforcers of the revolution, signaling internal dissent over the appropriate use of traditional structures in the revolutionary project and highly debating over how to reconcile customary authority with socialist principles.

As per Abbas, Soilihi screamed at him saying, "Do you not realize that I have visions, great visions? That is, I who guide our destiny?" (Lamb, 1982, p.113)

In this period, Western Journalist Lamb suggests that the revolution became "the *periode norie*, as it became known, had begun… (Lamb, 1982, p.111)." Lamb also makes the claims that Soilihi had a breakdown from the pressures of presidency and being the Mongozi exceeded his abilities. Yet, contrary to his own documentation, Lamb infantizes and speaks in racist terms as "[t]he Comoros became Soilihi's personal toy, and like a child with a new Christmas present, he played and experimented and manipulated, ending one game and starting another whenever he became bored (Lamb,1982, p.112)." To many of his self-conflicting journalship, Lamb wanted a story to create shock and horror for Western audiences.

Lamb also suggests that the visions experienced by the Mongozi were induced by substances, specifically Valium and hashish. Among these visions was a prophetic image foretelling that a man accompanied by a black dog would bring an end to both Soilihi's life and the revolution, illustrating the possible interplay of hallucinatory experience, ritual interpretation, and political anxiety within the revolutionary context.

Dietsche

Then Came a Pirate and His Black Dog

I must preface that this work was to delineate the Secular and Social Republic to Western Marxists, to include Ali Soilihi as part of the collection of Afrikan and international socialist leaders, as well as to challenge and criticize many sensational writings about the events of Denard coup on May 13,1978. These writings seek to create and perpetuate white man's burden, eurocentrism, racism, and imperialism. As much as I craved all information about the revolution, many documents are unreliable and non-usable because of their sources specifically to the anti-Soilihist coup. Many books and websites portray Bob Denard as the romantic pirate as the righter of the so-called socialist wrong of revolutions in Africa. Denard should be portrayed as a more sinister Colonel Kurz or as an "errand boy" like Captain Willard in *Apocalypse Now*. Many resources present Denard meddling of African democratic, popularist, nationalist, and anti-imperialist revolutions, but do not attack Denard directly for these usurping crimes.

One great vacuum of knowledge is about the French bringing ylang-ylang to Comoros as a cash crop and its connection to the revolution. Vanilla and ylang-ylang were major exports and one of the reasons for France to control Comoros. Paris, the perfumery of the world, world famous for Chanel No. 5 and the active ingredient is ylang-ylang, and in 1974 the export reached one hundred tons from Comoros as the world's leading producer (Bellantan,2022). What documents there is, there is one mention of the nationalization of these plants or the plants as unsustainable in a collective society. During the revolution, these products were in the hands of the state and in control in the auspices of the "Comore-Denrées". This is the only mention of revolutionary structure of ylang-ylang. Scholar of Comoros,

Lou Bellantan makes no other mention if ylang-ylang was left to go to the weeds or used for anything internally (Bellantan,2022). It seems that while the nationalization of ylang-ylang was acknowledged during the revolution, further details about its management or use within the revolutionary context are not readily available in the provided information.

My hypothesis was if the revolution stopped export of ylang-ylang, this would have greatly fettered French Chanel interests. The exiled Comorian bourgeoisie had a market reason to reestablish an independent but capitalist Comoros. This meant that there was a need for Bob Denard and Ahmend Abdallah to resume French ylang-ylang exports. As of publication, there is no record of Chanel through intermediaries asking for a solution. This is conjecture, but because of the revolution in Comoros threatening French ylang-ylang profits and losing a citadel in Francophone world, this threat would be enough for France to call for an invasion. There is also a South Africa connection to reinstall capitalism in Comoros thereby restoring the Air Comoros base in Moroni as a stop-over base for apartheid planes going from Pretoria to Saudi Arabia (Terril, 1986). After a successful counter revolution coup, spice trade plantations specifically for French colonialism and apartheid aid would resume.

Whether Soilihi was fully prepared for a counterrevolutionary coup remains uncertain, but in France, opponents of the revolution were actively plotting its downfall. Wealthy Comorians residing in Marseille, together with French imperialist elements, conspired with Bob Denard to remove Soilihi from power. Ex-President Ahmed Abdallah, based in Paris, and a cadre of exiled Comorian bourgeois politicians, supported by French intelligence, coordinated with Denard to facilitate Abdallah's return to power. According to Denard, the operation was overseen by René Journiac, who acted as a broker in his capacity as a member of the Élysée. At this time, Denard had recently led a failed coup attempt in Benin in 1977, demonstrating both his persistence and readiness to engage once more in Comoros— the site of his successful coup in 1975. This sequence of events underscores the transnational dimensions of the counterrevolution and highlights the convergence of exiled political actors, mercenary forces, and state intelligence in undermining revolutionary regimes.

From the website Orspatranostria.com, a site dedicated to Denard's own cult of fanaticism, Denard's words from his "Corsair of the Republic" presents a memoir about his actions against Comoros, Benin, Mauritania, and other places he usurped. Regarding Operation Atlantis, we have the words of Denard detailing his actions, his thoughts of Soilihi and how the operation will be bankrolled:

> "Ali Soilhi is indeed leading a policy that is more and more harmful to his country. Under cover of reforming it, of putting an end to feudalism, it flouts old traditions and leads its people towards the precipice. I end up going to the arguments of those who want to bring down his regime. When Saint-Hubert asks me how I intend to finance this operation, I point out to him that it is his friends, President Abdallah in the lead, who must put their hand sink their pockets first (Denard, second paragraph)."

Denard indicates that they believe individuals associated with Ahmed Abdallah should provide financial support for this endeavor. This suggests a potential collaboration or support from external actors in efforts to challenge Soilih's regime.

The coup finally happened in May 1978, of which Operation Atlantis was launched with the boat L' Antinea. Denard's piratic team was created with fifty mercenaries. After leaving Lorient, passing between Canary Islands, Cape of Good Hope, and bound for Moroni. To cover up the operation, Denard created an offshore seismic and geophysical research company to pretend to be studying oceanography when they were en route to Tierra del Fuego. Adding injury more injury, Bob Denard, took along his German Shepherd dog when he invaded, to add the prophecy of Soilihi knowing that a man and a black dog would come to kill him.

On May 13, 1978, the ship L'Antinéa landed on the beach of Itsandra, on the coast of Ngazidija/Grande Comoros. Many documents exclude the fact that Denard's mercenaries murdered at least two hundred Moissy in those hours. In 4 hours, Moroni then passes under the control of the 50 or so mercenaries and Ali Soilihi is taken prisoner. There is much Eurocentrism regarding how Denard so-called "liberated Comorian people". In this view, Denard returned power to the white power structures vis a vis the French. Fanon would say the infamous quote "Here I am Master" as a white savior belief that the Africans need to be saved from their own liberation (Fanon,1967, p.17)."

What happened to Ali Soilihi during the coup that annulled the Secular and Social Republic continues to be mysterious, ambiguous, ambivalent and full of myth. Regarding Soilihi's death as cited in Peterson (2021), is only another part of the long tradition of the "founding myths" in nation-states. What can be established is that the coup abruptly ended the brief three-year period during which Comorians had the opportunity to shape their own imaginative and autonomous destiny. Yet, in many accounts, the population was portrayed as being 'liberated' from Ali Soilihi, reflecting a contested memory of the revolution. This duality—between the loss of a fledgling socialist experiment and the narrative of liberation—highlights the complexities of popular perception, the manipulation of political discourse, and the fragility of revolutionary legitimacy in postcolonial Comoros.

> "May 13 marks the end of a political imagination, thanks to the support of a band of mercenaries, known to be the valets of the French state. But as if that were not enough, they had to kill the mastermind of this revolution, so that everyone remembers the lesson. Never again is such madness! And this is how Ali Soilihi died in detention on May 29, 1978, assassinated (stabbed? riddled with bullets?) in front of a strangely joyful population (Giachino,2021, para 6)."

Denard implies that Soilihi's death was deliberately orchestrated to serve as a warning to others, conveying the broader message that revolutionary initiatives of this kind would not be tolerated in the future. Across novels, folklore, bourgeois intrigue, and even contemporary platforms such as Twitter, the question continues to haunt Comorians: 'What happened to Ali Soilihi?' Travel writer Weinberg highlights the persistent uncertainty surrounding the circumstances of Soilihi's death, raising questions about which version of events can be considered authentic and underscoring the ways in which memory, narrative, and political agendas intersect in the ongoing construction of historical truth:

> "[w]ho knows if it was true? I was fast coming to accept that Comorians love to tell stories, and they don't really respect the distinction between truth and fiction. In such a small country, stories spread like Chinese whispers, often ending up distorted. They would be repeated so many times that people ended up believing them (Weinberg,1994, p.84)."

This quote reflects skepticism about the reliability of information in Comoros, suggesting that stories and rumors are often embellished or distorted as they are passed on. Weinberg implies that in a small country like Comoros, information spreads quickly and can become exaggerated or altered in the process. This leads to a blurring of the lines between truth and fiction, with people ultimately believing the stories they hear, regardless of their accuracy.

Like many revolutionary leaders that died before their time, Soilihi's death as per Denard is "[i]n fact, the circumstances of his death remain obscure, and some see the hand of the mercenaries. He will be killed a few days later: officially during an escape attempt" (Denard, para 56).

Taking cues that many stories and shadows exist at the same time and trying to conceptualize one truth about what happened on May 13th, we will focus on presenting the main hypothesis of each one. Noting that all of them, with the exception of pro-Soilhist versions, come with a Eurocentric, paternalistic racism that has perpetuated the mistruths.

There is not any journalistic objectivity to writing on revolutions. It is always a hard question of how much it is to believe the bourgeois lies of socialist revolution. Yet many of these versions could be philosophically polyphonic and happening at the same time and not.

Bellatan Version

As Editor of Dghanzi Books, a pro-Soilihist publisher, Lou Bellantan in an email interview wrote on what happened on May 13, 1978:

> "May 13th At 3.a.m on that day, the mercenaries landed on the beach of Itsandra and rushed in 3 directions. On that day Ali Swalih (sp) was toppled from his power. This coup d'état came as a surprise to everybody except to Ali himself. A few days before, he had met his militants and warned them that a coup was imminent. He had been informed by his intelligence service. To avoid bloodshed, he had sent his best troops to the next island of Ndzouani. In the same outlook, he said to his friends and militia men: 'Mind you! If you hear the Head of State has succeeded in fleeing, then you'll have to fight; but if you hear he has been captured and is a prisoner, then you'll have

> to lay arms and surrender (Bellatan, 2022, para 12)."

Surprisingly, Soilihi had been aware of the impending coup, as he had been informed by his intelligence service. In anticipation of the coup and to prevent bloodshed, he had sent his best troops to the neighboring island of Ndzouani/Anjouran. Soilihi had instructed his supporters that if they heard he had successfully fled, they should fight, but if they heard he had been captured and was a prisoner, they should surrender.

Continuing on Bellatan's version, Bob Denard ran up straight to the Presidency building in Mdrodjou and found Al Soilihi in bed with his two girl bodyguards:

> "On May 13, 1978, Ali Swalih was overthrown. This is a surprise for everyone, except for him! Because he followed the operation of the mercenaries and warned his supporters and activists of the imminence of the coup. He expects the arrival of the mercenaries and sends his best troops to Ndzouani to avoid confrontation and a bloodbath. He does more; he gives precise instructions to his militants: "If you learn that the Head of State is on the run, then you will have to fight. But, if you learn that he has been taken prisoner, then you must lay down your arms and surrender." Another way to avoid civil war and deadly battles! Because Bob Denard arrives at 3 a.m. and

goes straight to Mdrodjou where he finds Ali in his bed! (para 23)."

Regarding Soilihi's murder, as per Bellantan, Soilihi was shot trying to escape, murdered Che-style in prison, and other accounts say he was stabbed to death. There is also the only mentioning of Soilihi being diagnosed with cancer:

"On May 29th, 1978, At about 4 a.m. Ali who was a prisoner since May 13th was stabbed to death. The personalities who had financed the mercenaries and ordered the coup d'état had been welcomed triumphally on their arrival in Moroni on May 21st. During the following week they had gathered to reach an agreement upon what was to be done with their prisoner. It was decided by a narrow majority to put him to death. It was a secret meeting. The jury didn't know Ali was doomed to die because of his throat cancer. Ali had no doubt about his lot. He knew he would be killed and accepted his fate (Bellantan, 2022, para 13)."

Bellantan's account appears to be the most reliable, largely because he is openly pro-Soilihist and thus aligned with those sympathetic to Soilihi's revolutionary project. In contrast, other accounts—produced by travel journalists, less rigorous reporters, and reactionary scholars tend to be less substantiated and are often shaped by external biases or limited understanding of the local political and social context.

Hebditch and Connor Version

From an uncited source that perpetuates sensationalized versions of the "Soilihi and watching porn" version. Hebdicth and Connor (2017) state that "Saleh" was relaxing in the presidential bedroom with three naked schoolgirls. They were smoking marijuana and watching an 8-mm porn film projected on the wall when the door burst open. Standing in the doorway was Bob Denard. After killing Soilihi, the story goes that Denard drapes Soilihi's body on a jeep and drives around (Hebditch and Connor,2017). From where the source of this tale is, only reinforces that fable is part of the Comorian tradition. There is also the detail in Hebditch and Connor's story that unlike the other versions of the coup, there is detail of Ali Soilihi's tombstone.

Time Magazines Version

In an article by *Time Magazine* called "Comoro Islands: A Man and his Dog" published on Aug. 21, 1978, adds to the "Madman of Moroni" version including the inhuman massacre against Moissy by Denard's mercenaries. It is also in this version there is mentioning of the bringing along the German shepherd:

> "Many Comorans speculated that Soilih had flipped out and gone psychosomatic after a fortuneteller warned that he would be overthrown by a man with a mutt. On the other hand, the stocky dictator may have

dreamed up the idea while smoking hashish, an activity that seemed to take up much of his time.

Soilihi was reportedly still under the influence of hashish one night in May when thirty white mercenaries landed stealthily on a beach near Moroni, the capital city. They were led by French-born Colonel Robert Denard, then fifty years old, a notorious soldier of fortune whose military career over the previous 23 years had left bloody marks across numerous African conflicts.

In accordance with ominous foretelling, Denard was accompanied by a German shepherd. Within a matter of hours, Denard and his group had neutralized Soilihi's bodyguards, placed the president under arrest, and received the surrender of the Comoran army—a ragtag force of roughly two hundred men that did not fire a single shot.

The coup sparked a week of public celebration, which intensified upon the announcement that Soilihi had died while 'trying to escape' (*Times Magazine*, 1978).

This version describes speculation among Comorians about Ali Soilihi's mental state and the circumstances surrounding his overthrow. Some believed that Soilihi may have become paranoid after a fortuneteller warned him about being overthrown by a man with a dog, while others suggested that his use of hashish may have influenced his behavior. The text then recounts the events of the coup led by Colonel Robert Denard, who was accompanied by a German shepherd, as predicted by the fortuneteller.

Lamb's Version

Eurocentric journalist Lamb (1982) writes the personified pro-colonial "white man's burden"-type sophism in the reactionary travelogue *The Africans*. Reading his travelogue, it would seem that Lamb drafted this story to sensationalize and promote the racist and white supremacist theory that People of Color and the overall decolonization of Africa resulted in people not knowing how to rule themselves.

Trying to sift through Lamb and to figure out what is real is never-ending. One of the questionable claims that appear to be groundless and dubious in the Lamb article is that Comorians had T-shirts made with Denard as the liberator (Lamb, 1978).

Without citations, primary documents, or citing his sources, the journalist Lamb gives a similar but another account that includes Olacharry Christian, a French shipping agent drinking brandy with Soilihi. Christian, it seems, was the instigator who told Denard that Soilihi had fallen asleep drunk. Then, Soilihi was captured, and later shot by guards two weeks afterward.

In this version, Denard put Soilihi's body on his rover and took it to Soilihi's mother and sister. Denard said "[h]ere is Ali Soilihi," dragging the body off to the ground. Denard added that "[i]f you need some of my men to dig a hole, I will get them. But I do not want a lot of people at the burial (Lamb, 1982. p. 116)." Later, Ali Soilihi's body was placed in a cement coffin, with his name either scratched or graffitied onto it. Unlike Hebditch and Connor, Lamb relies on primary sources gathered through direct interviews, providing a closer and potentially more reliable perspective on the events surrounding Soilihi's death. This approach allows for a nuanced reconstruction of both the physical treatment of Soilihi's body and the broader social and political reactions to his demise, highlighting the value of firsthand testimony in documenting contested historical episodes.

In another enigmatic turn, Lamb reports in a Washington Post article dated October 30, 1978, that Denard's men found Soilihi intoxicated on brandy at the time of the coup. In the aftermath, the coup provoked strong condemnation from African leaders. Idi Amin reportedly declared his desire 'to throw Denard into the Indian Ocean,' while socialist leaders such as Albert René of Seychelles and Julius Nyerere of Tanzania also expressed dismay over the ascension of the new government and the role of mercenaries. The depth of this regional disdain was such that both René and Nyerere urged the Organization of African Unity (OAU) to take measures against Abdallah's government, reflecting widespread concern over external interference and the destabilization of a revolutionary socialist regime in Comoros.

Masawai Version

According to sources from the Comorian journal Masawai, Ali Soilihi was battling throat cancer while simultaneously seeking to ensure that the revolution would have the best chance of success in his absence. An excerpt from Collective, published by Djahazi and titled 'The Shooting Star Shines Forever,' appeared in Masawai and included interviews reflecting on Soilihi's death. In this account, Soilihi was acutely aware of the plots surrounding him even as he faced a terminal illness (Masawai, 2023).

Similarly, JC Favetto notes, in line with earlier observations, that Soilihi understood he was a condemned man but nonetheless chose to send young students away, placing revolutionary principles above personal safety. On September 3, 1977, Soilihi personally greeted these students at Moroni Airport, demonstrating both his commitment to the cause and his awareness of the risks that lay ahead.

> "…looking unhappy, with tears in his eyes. He let me understand that he wasn't sure if we would see each other again and that he was counting on me a lot for the future. // A few days before our departure, he received me face to face, lying on his bed, because he was a little unwell. He had taken a look at the list of young people who were leaving to continue their studies abroad (a list he had requested from me a few days before this meeting) and said to me: 'You have chosen the best that I trained, to leave us, at a crucial moment in our history. I won't have time to train others.' he continued (*Masawai*, 2023, para 3)."

Among the students departing to study abroad was Youssouf Saïd Swalih, who was preparing to pursue studies in finance. At Moroni Airport, he shook hands with the Mongozi, an encounter that he later recalled with deep emotion. Youssouf felt instinctively that this would be the last time he would see the Mongozi alive, a premonition that underscored the precarious political climate of the time. His testimony also sheds light on the symbolic role of young people within Soilihi's revolution: they were not only beneficiaries of the state's investment in education abroad but also living embodiments of the revolution's imagined future, charged with carrying its ideals into new domains of knowledge and practice.

"I was lucky enough to be selected to go abroad for training in the field of finance. This gave me the opportunity to shake hands with the Mwongozi, for the last time, at the Mroni-Ikoni airport. He had specially traveled from Mwali to come and wish us a good trip. But this "Goodbye" was, ultimately, to turn out to be a "Farewell." That day we saw him in tears. It was following a question asked by the Radio-Komor journalist at the time, about the team which was going to leave the country to study abroad. He wanted to have the Guide's feeling about the continuity of the Revolution in which young people played the role of vanguard. In his response, as far as I remember, Ali said: "These young people are an integral part of my own body and their departure I feel as if I were losing part of my flesh. He said these words with great emotion. And added: "You leave today, some will come back to heal the wounds of others, but always stay united, never disperse." (Masawi, 2023, para 5)."

Even in his dying days, Soilihi was committed to the role of the youth, and the continuation of the revolution. A close activist and associate of Ali Soilihi, S. Chanudet writes about the last weeks of Soilihi and the revolution. It is in this statement that Ali Soilihi gave instructions on what happens if he lives or dies:

"Ali knew he was going to fail because I remember the last weeks before we left for Ndzouani. We were given instructions telling us that, for 4 weeks, we should not sleep outside // but remain vigilant. There were thoughts of an imminent coup d'état. Ali himself had said to his loved ones: We

> still have a dangerous month! This is the turning point of the Revolution, as if reaching Do'mba. If we pass this milestone, we will have achieved our political objective. But if, one day, you learn that the Head of State is captured, then you will have to lay down your arms. If, on the contrary, you are told that the Head of State managed to escape, then you will have to resist (Masawi, 2023, para 6)."

In the weeks leading up to the events at Ndzouani, Ali Soilihi conveyed to his associates a sense of impending danger and the possibility of a coup d'état. He instructed them to remain vigilant and avoid sleeping outside for four weeks.

Soilihi himself expressed a belief that they were entering a critical phase of the revolution, akin to reaching a pivotal milestone. He indicated that if he were to be captured, they should surrender, but if he managed to escape, they should continue to resist.

This demonstrates Soilihi's awareness of the precariousness of his position and his strategic thinking in preparing for potential challenges to his leadership.

Ex-revolutionary Ahamada Mfwahaïa recalls that, upon Ali Soilihi's capture, the leader did not appear to be a failure as a revolutionary. His composure and commitment suggested a continued dedication to the revolutionary cause.

However, it soon became evident that the Mongozi had been killed by Denard's mercenaries, a brutal act that underscored the lethal determination of the counterrevolutionary forces and marked a decisive end to Soilihi's leadership.

> "Mohamed Taki called us, the young people of Hamahamé, and said to us: "Do you know what happened? " " No! ". "Ali Swalih was killed. When the decision was made, me, Mohamed Ahmed, Rachid Mbaraka and Omar Tamou refused. There were 5 of us who refused but 6 of them agreed (Masawi, 2023, para 6)."

Mohamed Taki informed the young people of Hamahamé about Ali Soilihi's death, revealing that a decision had been made regarding his fate. Taki, along with Mohamed Ahmed, Rachid Mbaraka, and Omar Tamou, were among those who refused to agree with the decision. Despite their opposition, six others supported the decision. Despite discrepancy of whether Ali Solihi was killed by running away or stabbed, it is impossible to know which one of the truths are real. In this document the death of the Mongozi also hits his faithful, his loved ones:

> 'Colonel B. Denard was accompanied by Commander Ahmed Mohamed and the Minister of Information, Hadji Hassanali; They came here, very happy: "Did everything go well? Was the package delivered in good condition? And on the day of his burial, there were many of them. They were there to keep watch and to check that they were burying this "communist dog" and that they were not being filmed or photographed. Because there, we would

have seen that he had indeed been murdered. There was even an agent, Lava, when we washed the body in the morning. There were few people at the funeral. Terror reigned in Chouwani. There could be ten people, the family only. Besides, they didn't let anyone near the place. The first project, broadcast by radio, came from the Moufti; the body had to be thrown into the sea. I don't know who refused. So, they were afraid that we would discover the truth. They had to change his clothes which were saturated [soggy] with blood. They had put other clothes on him but these, again, were soaked in blood. They had wrapped the body in a blanket which was stained with blood, but only on the inside (Masawi, 2023, para 9)."

With this version, the morning of May 29th in Chouwani, Saïd Habibou recalls the events surrounding Ali Soilihi's death. Upon hearing neighbors crying outside, they learn of Ali Soilihi's murder. Subsequent radio reports claim Ali Soilihi tried to escape and was shot. Around 10 a.m., Ali Soilihi's body arrives wrapped in a yellow blanket, wearing familiar clothes. The Saïd Habibou assists in preparing the body, noticing two small holes in the chest from which blood flowed when lifted. They wash Ali Soilihi body with others, despite objections from a bystander. Mercenaries instructed by Denard ensure privacy during the process. Saïd Habibou with others, conducts a Muslim-style washing of Ali's body before burial. Another journalist discusses how Soilihi had to disappear because of dangerous he was to the French.

In the same document, Saïd Habibou known as "Philo" recalls the remorse over Ali Soilihi being shot while escaping:

"On the morning of May 29, in Chouwani, the grandmother gave me tea which I refused. One of the young people who were there, the son of Ali's cousin, Pigeon's brother, Swalih Mzé, had tea and left for school; he was in 5th grade. I was in 6th grade. I said, "I'm not going to school today!" " I remained at home; I was sad. And it struck the grandmother: "This child, it's true! He has always been attached to Ali! And, suddenly, around 8 a.m., we heard the neighbors crying outside – in Chouwani, for the vast majority of residents, Ali was their child – I went to the door, and I learned that Ali had been murdered. We turned on the radio and learned that Ali had tried to escape and had been shot. Around 10 a.m., the body was brought in, and I was there, with his mother and sister. We prepared a place, and they came to lay the body, wrapped in a yellow blanket, and wearing his clothes: a white t-shirt, his jacket, slightly yellow pants, and brown shoes. I took off the clothes myself, but the T-shirt was full of blood; I tried to wash this T-shirt, but I couldn't, there was so much blood; I buried him in the yard. I kept the jacket and pants to this day. And even, the cover is still there. I went to call the purifier (mhossa mwili), Hamadi Mwandzé, I brought him to the house; with Kombo who now works at the post office, we washed the body; there was Kombo, my father, Souf Bourhane, Mohamed Ahamada, myself… In all, there were 8 of us. Others were at the door… It was then that I saw two holes through which the blood was flowing. flowed when the body was lifted; on the other hand, when the body was placed, the blood did not flow. There were two very small holes in the chest, on the right and left, but nothing in the back. I also noticed that there were black dots at the orifice. There wasn't much blood in the blanket; it was especially the T-shirt that was saturated. B. Denard told two mercenaries to stay, so that no one would come and disturb us, he said. Besides, someone tried to intervene, saying: "He is an unbeliever! You should not wash your body! The two mercenaries sent him away. We washed his body, Muslim style, and went to bury him… (Masawi,2023, para 6)."

With this version, the morning of May 29th in Chouwani, the narrator recalls the events surrounding Ali Soilihi's death. Despite initially refusing tea, the narrator remains at home, feeling sad. Upon hearing neighbors crying outside, they learn of Ali Soilihi's murder. Subsequent radio reports claim Ali Soilihi tried to escape and was shot.

Around 10 a.m., Ali Soilihi's body arrives wrapped in a yellow blanket, wearing familiar clothes. The narrator assists in preparing the body, noticing two small holes in the chest from which blood flowed when lifted. They wash Ali Soilihi's body with others, despite objections from a bystander. Mercenaries instructed by B. Denard ensure privacy during the process.

The narrator, along with others, conducts a Muslim-style washing of Ali's body before burial. Another journalist discusses how Soilihi had to disappear because of how dangerous he was to the French.

On June 12, 1978, journalist E. Ramarou summarized a eulogy in solidarity:

"Ali Soilihi, the former Leader of the Revolution, had to disappear; he had to die because he was too dangerous. He was tough, intrepid, frank, a player. He identified himself with the revolution. He had "everything in his head." He captivated, with his smile, his eloquence, his energy, his verve. He administered, consulted, observed. At night, he thought, made plans, devoured books. He galloped ahead of the Revolution. The young people followed, the people did not always understand. His enemies took advantage of it. They have dealt with the most urgent matter: that at least the beast dies and, with it, if possible, its ideas. Ali had spared Ahmed Abdallah. The man from France delivered him to the executioners.

History will not forget (Maswawi, 2023, para 9)."

Soilihi had to meet his end because he posed a significant threat. He was bold, fearless, outspoken, and deeply involved in the revolution. With his charisma, intelligence, and tireless dedication, he led the movement forward, often ahead of his time. While he inspired the youth, the broader populace sometimes struggled to grasp his vision. Exploiting this, his enemies deemed him too dangerous to be left alive, aiming to silence both him and his ideas. Despite sparing Ahmed Abdallah, Ali Soilihi ultimately fell victim to betrayal, delivered into the hands of his executioners. History will remember this dark chapter. On May 13, 1991, Salim Himidi looked back on the period:

"The taking of the levers of control of our country, by B. Denard and his outlaws, largely contributed to the early rehabilitation of Ali Swalih, as Leader (Mwongozi), redeemer, midwife of a more just society and more united. It is up to those responsible to take the proper measure of Ali Swalih's unfinished work (Masawi, 2023 para 11)."

The seizure of power by Bob Denard and his mercenary group prompted a significant reevaluation of Ali Soilihi's leadership. In retrospect, Soilihi came to be seen not merely as a political figure, but as a visionary leader, a redeemer, and a catalyst for a more just and cohesive society. His revolutionary project, though abruptly interrupted, continues to resonate as an aspirational model for governance and social reform. It is now incumbent upon current leaders to acknowledge Soilihi's unfinished legacy and to take meaningful steps toward realizing the vision of equity, national cohesion, and popular empowerment that he championed.

There are many other slightly differed versions of the Mongozi's arrest and death. But one is certain, that Ali Soilihi's revolution was overturned and Soilihi was killed by Denard's mercenaries. The use of mercenaries post-Soilihism would continue. Comoros is unique that it contains mercenaries as the main source of power for many decades. Furthermore, as per Mukonoweshuro, " above all, the Comoros is unique in the sense that it is the only known state in contemporary Africa in which a 'sovereign' government has been installed and maintained by a group of mercenary free- booters who struck a formal relationship with the government and became an integral part of the supposedly legitimate state institutions (Mukonoweshuro,1990, p. 55)."

The statement highlights a distinctive aspect of the Comoros Islands' political history, specifically regarding the role of mercenaries in establishing and sustaining a government. Yet we do not know for certain a specific truth that happened to the Mongozi, but we do know the revolution was destroyed by mercenaries that continued to be a unique and terrible part of the history of Comoros. This legacy continued to hinder Comoros experiencing unique political dynamics, including instances of mercenary involvement in governance up to the 2000's.

Post-Mortems and Myths

> "By murdering Mongzozi Ali Soilihi, they murdered the entire Comorian people"
> --*Nouvelle Génération Soilihiste*

Whichever specific truth(s) ended the life of Mongozi Ali Soilihi, the revolution was over and Denard put Ahmed Abdallah back into power. Abdallah again claimed the title of president and named Bob Denard as commander of the five hundred strong Presidential Guard.

As part of the bourgeoise mercenary-supported regime, Abdallah's new government immediately nullified Soilihi's constitution in a dramatic reversal. Islam was again paramount in Comorian society—at least on the surface.

A few of the key changes made to the ruling structure of Comoros were changing the voting age back to eighteen, set up autonomous governorships, and set in place a mechanism by which the presidency was secured.

The Abdullah 1978 constitution made sure that the supreme court, national council, and island councils were staffed with enough loyalists to maintain control. The president not only selected his own Prime Minister but also had a great deal of influence in selecting the Supreme Court and National Council. Functionaries nominated by the president had a disproportionate amount of power to the governors and the elected legislative councils on each island.

Aboubacar Said Salim, a former member of the Democratic Front (FD), a counter-revolutionary group which was opposed to Soilihi wrote from France describing the Denard and his men as "angels." Salim writes that "[n]obody wanted to fall back into the revolution. Young people had an interest in keeping a low profile because they felt that they had committed abuse. This is the speech we heard: 'They are angels, not mercenaries.' (Giachino, 2021, para 25)."

To replace the Moissy, the mercenaries forged and trained the 500-man Presidential Guard. The GP was divided into three companies and commanded by mercenary officers. This real state within another state was the GP and was recognizable by its black uniforms. The GP was an entity completely loyalty to Abdallah (Denard, year unknown).

From 1978 onward, Bob Denard effectively established the Comoros as his rear base, shaping the political trajectory of the islands for more than a decade. The period from the coup that destroyed the revolution on May 13, 1978, to November 26, 1989, marked the entirety of Ahmed Abdallah's second presidency, which ultimately ended with his death at the hands of another mercenary.

Consequently, the modern history of the Comoros during this period is inextricably linked to the activities of Bob Denard, whose interventions repeatedly influenced the islands' political stability.

Amidst this turbulent era, Ali Soilihi's revolutionary project continued to attract scholarly and popular interest, ensuring that his historical and theoretical legacy remained a point of reflection and debate within Comorian memory and postcolonial studies

Legacy of Mongozi

"Each generation must discover its mission, fulfill it or betray it, in relative opacity (Fanon, 1967, xxxi)."

"His (Soilihi) idea was to remain in the Comorian History as a myth and a martyr (Bellatan, 2022)."

Comorian history and Soilihi are very much alive and connected in myth and historicism. The revolutionary legacy of Ali Soilihi was seen by many as said by Giachino (2005d) calling Soilihi the "[m]isunderstood visionary (para 6)." Lamb interviewed Soilihi's mother years after the coup and writes she said that "does not believe all you hear about Ali Soilihi; my son was a good boy (Lamb,1982, p. 111)." This statement highlights the subjective nature of historical interpretation and the importance of considering multiple perspectives when forming judgments about individuals and their actions. It also underscores the complexity of human beings, as individuals may have different facets to their personalities and legacies depending on who is perceiving them and from what vantage point.

Soilihi's mother continues:

"Ali would come every month to bring me food and a few francs, and he was always talking about what he wanted to something

> for his people. He said Communism was best for a poor country like this. He said experiments with it failed in Tanzania and all over Africa, but he was going to make it work and all the world would look to Comoros (Lamb,1982, p. 111)."

By mentioning Soilihi's acknowledgment of past failures of communism in other African countries like Tanzania, his mother acknowledges that Soilihi was aware of the challenges associated with implementing such ideologies in practice. However, Soilihi's confidence in his ability to make communism work in the Comoros and his belief that the world would take notice reflects his ambition and determination to transform his nation.

Soilihi was the Mongozi, the guide of the revolution, which grew to be the "Mythical Leader, redeemer, midwife of a fairer and united society, avenger of all injustices and inequalities" (Arm, 2019, para 1). This omniscient view was indeed to perpetuate Soilihi as a Comorian Messiah, myth-creator ethos, and the fixer of Comorian oppression.

To just simplify the revolution as led by Soilihi who was merely a rabid "anarchist in jeans" and a Muslim infidel who defamed Islam in making socialism just collective misery, would be a serious error.

The three years of Comorian socialism were the only free, democratic, and sovereign years of its history to date. Broken from the chains of French imperialism, racism, the Francophone circle, and on the road to breaking the tethers of gender exploitation from the Grande Marriages, and the use of Comoros as a water station and a cheap source of materials, Comoros tried to walk on its own feet:

"Ali Soilih attempted what no politician has sought to achieve in these islands to date: to build a nation. He thought that by pushing his fellow citizens to the limit, the new man would emerge from the feudal brothel and from the expectations aroused by his egalitarian logic. Building a nation also meant laying the foundations of a common identity. A reference base! Beyond the flag and the hymns of dignity, the Mongoze (Mongozi) undertook to shake up the habits and customs of his contemporaries, by "shaking" the ancestral legacies, by confronting them with the reality of the world and by inscribing them in a new imaginary, where hope meets the audacity of the citizen. The imagination! A magic word that the Mongoze manipulated with great genius. Ali Soilih invited his constituents to question the common memory, favoring not a fixed and backward-looking expression of tradition, but rather a living and popular form of cultural identity, authorizing the birth of the Comorian nation in the most modern absolute (unknown source)."

This passage provides a comprehensive overview of Ali Soilihi's ambitious nation-building efforts in the Comoros Islands. It emphasizes Soilihi's unique approach to governance, characterized by a blend of ideological vision, social reform, and cultural revitalization.

Central to Soilihi's nation-building project was the revitalization of Comorian culture and heritage. He recognized the importance of cultural identity in fostering national unity and encouraged a dynamic interpretation of tradition that resonated with contemporary realities.

Soilihi's leadership style was characterized by boldness and innovation. He skillfully employed the power of imagination to inspire his constituents and instill a sense of hope for the future. Through his visionary leadership, he sought to shape a new societal paradigm grounded in progress and collective empowerment.

In a series of many articles in the Peking Review, Soilihi is recognized as the "father of the Comorian state" and the article publishes the problems with the new state:

> "Soilihi is the father of the Comorian state and of its international recognition, which he bequeathed in spite of himself to Ahmed Abdallah and his successors. Abroad, he obtained recognition of the independence of the four islands of the archipelago by the United Nations (UN), membership in the Organization of the African Union (OAU, now AU), and forged ties with Muslim countries that led to membership in the Arab League. He brought the Mahoran question to the world stage and succeeded in having the French attitude condemned by most countries. He finally knew how to juggle with diplomacy to obtain aid and loans without giving up the sovereignty of

> the Comoros. The cooperation with China, which he started, is still continuing. Inside, he simply faced an unprepared independence and the abrupt departure of French technical assistance (Muzdalifa House, 2005, para 45). "

The portrayal of Ali Soilihi as a visionary leader who endeavored to transform the Comoros into a modern, cohesive and collective nation-state. His nation-building efforts were marked by a commitment to social justice, cultural revival, and imaginative leadership, leaving a lasting impact on the trajectory of Comorian history.

This unpublished poem called "On Ali Soilihi's Birthday" tries to summarize the socialist Comorian project:

> "Ali Soilihi is breathing before he breathes the candles out. he talks on around, about three years' worth of socialist work for Comoros. on how far his influence is on -far from Moroni, the volcanoes, Anjouran, Moheil, Comoros Grande, and on the Moissy. I will eat what Comrade Ali Soilihi gives me, that includes the ylang-ylang cake (Dietsche, unpublished poem)."

Regarding the Soilihist political legacy, numerous groups and nonprofits continue to carry forward various aspects of Soilihism, even though there is currently no formal Soilihist political party in the Comoros.

Fondation Mtsachiya (2018), whose motto is 'L'histoire est seule juge' ('History is the only judge'), notes on its website: 43 years already since he left us. Thankfully, his ideas and determination stayed with us' (Fondation Mtsachiya, 2018). The group Djawbu also openly claims the legacy of Ali Soilihi (Fondation Mtsachiya, 2018, para. 5).

It is likely that many other organizations and individuals embrace elements of Soilihism without explicitly identifying as Soilihist through the press or activist work. Some groups actively seek to continue the revolutionary project in Soilihi's name, preserving his vision and promoting the principles associated with his leadership.

Another website finds it essential to bring together some of the contributions devoted to this forgotten period of Comorian history. As per Ankili (2019) there are a plethora of pro-Soilihi articles that with titles such as the "Founding Father" and one called the "Memory of the Mongozi" writes that:

> "It is up to everyone to form a discourse on the revolutionary events that took place in the Comoros between January 1976 and May 1978. Today, historians have a duty to shed light on those who fought the feudal system for the benefit of a popular political and social revolution. She dreamed of principles of equality. From a status of Comorian – citizen – with a constitution and laws, written to banish a system of sharing of property, inherited from the feudal world and consolidated by colonialism. Here, then,

> is the progressive legacy of the Comorian revolution (Ankili,2019, para 10)."

This underscores the importance of recognizing and commemorating the revolutionary struggle in the Comoros as a pivotal moment in its history. It calls upon historians to illuminate the contributions and aspirations of those who championed the cause of political and social transformation, leaving behind a legacy of progressive change for future generations. The group *Nouvelle Generation Soiliste*. promoted Soilihism at a social justice rally and uploaded on YouTube and the NGS, the Revolutionary national anthem of Ali Soilihi and sung by relatives. In the Comoros, political power has become reticent to the pre-Soilihist times coalescing around personalities than actual change.

Many YouTubers have published speeches regarding Soilihi. Dododry published a speech in French titled " Ali Soilihi Mtsachioi speech on various points that are currently up to date in France" Yet other posts contain how "Ali Soilihi the Dictator" paradigm that claims: "I wonder why accuse Ali Soilihi of being a dictator. Follow this speech until the end you will understand very well that he is the only Comorian president who wanted to do something in this country. (Dododry,2012)." Ex-Comorian revolutionary at the time Dini Nassur writes "At the time, we didn't say 'dictator' but 'revolutionary. It was a period of block warfare. It is certain that if he proceeded like that today... Now we know the virtues of democracy... but in the context of the time, I cannot say that it was really a mistake that he did not there is no democratic freedom and liberalism. For him, it was development that would bring about democracy (Giachino,2005a, para. 9)."

It is crucial to understand the prevailing conditions and ideologies of the time to fully grasp why certain choices were made. While we may now see democracy as a fundamental value, it might not have been the prevailing belief or feasible option in the context of past revolutions or political movements. Soilihi may have prioritized what he believed would lead to progress or stability, even if it meant sacrificing bourgeoisie democratic principles. Evaluating historical figures and their decisions requires a nuanced understanding of the complexities of their times. Another ex-Comorian activist Mohammed Dossar calls the so-called dictatorship as "enlightened despotism."

Mohammad Dossar writes that "[h]e (Soilihi) practiced a kind of enlightened despotism. Soilihi showed the Comorians that they were not alone on earth. " Another veteran of the revolution Said Oiffir wrote that Soilihi" made them aware of certain injustices and gave rise to a nationalist feeling (Giachno,2005, para 8)."

Overall, Soilihi's legacy appears comparable to that of many African socialist leaders who confronted similar challenges in recently decolonized, revolutionary nationalist contexts. Like his counterparts, he sought to implement transformative policies in societies marked by entrenched traditional structures, limited state capacity, and external pressures, highlighting both the possibilities and vulnerabilities of socialist experimentation in postcolonial Africa.

he Moissy has been one of the most sensationalized aspects of the Comorian revolution. Moissy haven been written about in many travelogs, journals, and blog posts, regarding the Soilihist revolution.

As written in Mohamed Toihir's novel—*La République des Imberbes* (*The Republic of the Beardless*)—is a satirized depiction of Soilihi and the Moissy. Toihir's novel was a total synthesis of memory satirizing the revolution. L'Harmattan wrote a review in 1985 regarding the coup in the book, reinforcing the myths and legends of "Guigoz" (aka Ali Soilihi in the book).

Tohir writes that the "mercenaries have no problem dealing with the guards and capturing the president. He is drunk, lying on a sofa with two completely naked women. He surrendered without a struggle and was then imprisoned. The rest of the novel is Guigoz ruminating on Soilihi's life" (L'Harmattan, 1985, paragraph 5).

Overall, Toihir—as per L'Harmattan—writes that the book "may well have been intended as a satire and, occasionally, Toihir does stray into satire but most of the book is a vitriolic attack on Soilihi/Guigoz. It is interesting for most Westerners, who are ignorant of these events and, indeed, of the country as a whole" (L'Harmattan, 1985, paragraph 5).

For most Western readers who may not be familiar with the historical context or the country of Comoros, this text could serve as an introduction to the events and the individuals involved. It may provide insights into a lesser-known aspect of history and shed light on the complexities of political dynamics in the region.

Like the novel Land *of the Beardless*, other novels albeit from a Eurocentric conversative point of view have the Soilihi legacy. In a novel called "The Seducer" by Jan Kjærstad, describes a fictional story about a TV documentarian. The main character is a member of a Norwegian Socialist youth group that found a short-lived obsession as a Soilihist. The character "Jonas" receives a letter from Ali Soilihi for Jonas's support of socialist Comoros in the Olympics. So smitten with Soilihi's letter and praise, that Jonas showed the letter from Mongozi like a religious scroll and raised the revolutionary Comoros flag over the schoolhouse (Kjaerstand 1999). This is probably the only noted, albeit fictious beginnings of International Soilihism!

My Soilihism is Better than Yours: Elainou vs. Hassan Jaffar

"Me Elaniou's Response to Hassan Jaffar" and "Ali Soilihi or independence in the cistern of Elaniou: A Bad indictment against the regime of Ali Soilihi" are major documents discussing Soilihi and the revolution dealing with legacy. I have cited both regarding the cisterns and liberation from Grande Marriages. In 2003, Saïd Hassane Jaffar wrote in a pro-Soilihist polemic to Me Elaniou's book, "Ali Soilih, or Independence in the cistern of Elaniou: A Bad indictment against the regime of Ali Soilih". Said Hassane Jaffar criticizes the legacy of the official legacy-holders.

As such, I remind readers that the purpose of this work is not to seek a sophist "middle ground," nor to propose a compromise or synthesis between Said Hassane Jaffar and Elaniou. This book is written as combat literature for revolution. It is for Comorians themselves to reclaim their socialist heritage and struggle for the liberation of Maore/Mayotte. These two authors illustrate the dialectic of Comorian storytelling—a testament to how deeply narrative shapes the nation. Elaniou, as Jaffar suggests, is to be "read like good fiction" (Said Hassane Jaffar, 2003). Yet Jaffar also discredits Elaniou's famous book, regarding it as "the perpetuation of untruths and falsifications so honored regarding Ali Soilih and the revolution" (Said Hassane Jaffar, 2003, para. 10).

Said Hassane Jaffar continues:

> "This book, despite the use of well-identified actors and sometimes duly authenticated events, cannot depart from the literary genre prized by pamphleteers, caricaturists, polemicists... Literary genre likely to use, sometimes, rumors, gossip and slander peddled by the street, and especially by a media like "Radio Comores'', past master in the art of disinformation, manipulation and editing of the event. Conduct that I disapprove of and that I personally disapproved of at the time, and which was partly at the origin of my departure in 1979 from the official radio [1]. (Said Hassane Jaffar, 2003, paragraph 10)"

Even though Said Hassane Jaffar does not take an overtly revolutionary line in his thesis against Elaniou, nor does he explicitly write in Marxist terms, his position is nevertheless, grounded in a clear political orientation. The context of Jaffar's critique is unmistakably pro-Soilihist and pro-socialist. For Jaffar, the stakes of narrative are not merely literary; they are historical and political. By exposing the distortions in Elaniou's text, he implicitly affirms the necessity of preserving the revolutionary memory of Ali Soilih and the socialist project that was violently overthrown.

Jaffar continues that Elaniou's work is not a neutral contribution to historiography, but a strategic intervention meant to obscure, delegitimize, and ultimately erase the emancipatory legacy of Soilih. In dismantling this falsification, Jaffar aligns himself—whether consciously or not—with the broader struggle to reclaim Comorian socialism as a living force. His refusal to adopt Marxist terminology should not distract us from the materialist content of his critique: he understands the ideological function of narrative, and he insists that Comorians must confront politics embedded in their own stories. In this way, Jaffar's position, while couched in academic critique, is in fact a partisan act. It situates him within a lineage of intellectual combatants who refuse to allow colonial or reactionary discourse to dictate the memory of the revolution.

"Practically everything in Ali Soilih or independence in the cistern is questionable: the grandiloquent tone tainted with contempt, the preposterous and outrageous nicknames bordering on slander and defamation, tricked out to those who have the bad idea of belonging to the wrong camp (that of Ali Soilihi), truncated words taken out of context, diverted from their meaning, false semantic studies, specious comments, cookie-cutter formulas... Everything is put to use, to always push further, everything that directly or indirectly affects the hated regime. To venture, for example, to translate Hwendelea usoni, which literally means "to move forward" by "headlong flight," is to demonstrate intellectual dishonesty and manifest bad faith. (Jaffar, 2003, paragraph 5) (Radio Comores, AFP, RFI), August 2003.

This underscores the pervasive bias and misinformation that have long shaped the portrayal of Ali Soilih and the crucial years of Comorian independence. The persistence of these distortions is not accidental but reflects deliberate attempts to obscure the socialist aspirations of that moment. What is required, therefore, is not another repetition of colonial or reactionary narratives, but a more rigorous and consciously situated examination of this history—one that acknowledges its subjective dimensions while refusing the falsifications that have dominated too many accounts.

Me Elaniou's Response to Hassan Jaffar

Me Elaniou, author of Ali Soilih or Independence in the Cistern (Komedit), responded to the criticisms of journalist Saïd Hassane Jaffar by reducing the debate to questions of partisanship. Rather than addressing the substance of Jaffar's arguments, Elaniou dismisses him as a mere "Soilihist," as though this label alone discredits his analysis. This maneuver reveals Elaniou's position as not simply critical but openly counter revolutionary. Unlike others who at least attempt to veil their hostility with historical or scholarly pretenses, Elaniou's intervention offers little more than attacks on Jaffar's professional legitimacy, particularly his work on Radio Comoros. In doing so, he exposes the shallow ground upon which reactionary narratives often stand—relying not on serious engagement with revolutionary memory but on discrediting those who dare to defend it.

"The Ufwakuzi (radical) revolution was no exception. The one who wanted to do it, probably the only one who believed in it one day, died, the others suddenly disappeared from circulation. The soldiers threw down their arms. They were the first to betray. They didn't fight for a second. They fled before the mercenaries. They shamed the flag. Politicians, ministers, or others quickly turned their backs. We find them in all successive regimes, all of which, beginning of course with that of Abdallah, have stigmatized the crimes of Ufwakuzi. They settled down, they saved the furniture. Finally, the journalists, those who had the infamous task of incensing the Mongozi up to and including its craziest excesses, and who, afterwards, hid themselves, so as not to have to render accounts. Finally! Finally! They are starting to come to the surface! At least this book will have served that purpose (Elaniou, 2011, first paragraph)!"

This depiction reveals a landscape of widespread abandonment and opportunism in the aftermath of the socialist revolution. It suggests that many individuals and groups chose self-preservation over fidelity to their revolutionary ideals, leaving behind a legacy of betrayal, silence, and moral compromise. The very invocation of a book that claims to illuminate these issues points to the urgent need to expose and confront the truth about the revolution and its suppression. Yet much of Elaniou's monologue amounts to little more than conjecture, speculation without substantiating evidence. His references to "the cisterns" and alleged abuses by the Moissy lack credible grounding and serve instead as rhetorical weapons wielded against Saïd Hassane Jaffar—dismissed not as a serious thinker but caricatured as merely "the journalist." This tactic reveals less about the revolution itself than about the counter-revolutionary posture of those who prefer to obscure history with rumor and innuendo rather than engage with its concrete realities.

"Because the journalist who speaks has not yet told us why between 1975 and 1978, we only heard panegyrics on Radio-Comoros, and no news! Why he told us nothing about the cisterns, the atrocities of the Komando Mwasi (authors note sp of Moissy), the raids in the villages, why he dressed in gold and dreams the most infamous acts, such as the collectivization of land at double speed, the villainous ordinance lavish spending, the auto-da-fé that Hassan denies so strongly today! Why the judicial investigations were taking place live on the radio, the secrecy of the investigation having been definitively trampled on, etc. (Elaniou, second paragraph)."

The importance of journalistic integrity and the media's role in holding those in power accountable. It suggests that during this period in the Comoros, the media failed to fulfill its responsibility to provide accurate, impartial, and critical reporting, allowing propaganda and censorship to prevail. Hopefully, future generations of radicalized Comorians can relinquish the Comorian bourgeoisie, the World Bank, and United Nations to create a new socialist state. Somehow, they must make peace with the specter that is haunting them, that is the specter of Soilihism.

Cisterns Legacy is Not Just for Water Anymore, Example in Oral Tradition

The use of cisterns as prisons had been a key source of debate and discussion regarding the legacy of Soilihism. This debate on hearsay and myth has become one of the key acid tests of how to remember the revolution. Many revolutionary veterans remember alleged counterrevolutionaries locked up in cisterns, along with the social humiliation of feudal-bourgeoise supporters. When analyzing Solihism and revolution, the zeitgeist of oral story telling/tradition are always the juxtaposition of truth.

> " Certainly, the Comoros are a country of oral tradition. But that does not exempt them from resorting to modern means of communication, including the written word, and even the audiovisual press. Cistern book recreates bourgeoisie ethnics. This book, despite the use of well-identified actors and sometimes duly authenticated events, cannot depart from the literary genre prized by pamphleteers, caricaturists, polemicists... (Weinberg,1994, p. 67)."

The importance of critically engaging with modern communication methods while cautioning against the perpetuation of harmful narratives or divisions in literature and media. It encourages a thoughtful approach to representation and discourse, particularly in a society with a diverse cultural heritage like the Comoros.

This is also the age-old debate of the use of violence, and imprisonment of class enemies, specifically in Global South anti-colonial liberation movements. As per Fanon (1967), the use of such terror is intricately part of the anti-colonial revolution. In this case, Soilihi and the revolution, had to break asunder centuries of feudal sultan misrule, the top-down bureaucracy of French deputies, and the years of misgovernment by post-independence serfdom by vestiges of royalty. Many remember the Moissy with a megaphone announcing class enemies and counterrevolutionaries of prisoners alleged crimes to the masses. YouTube has been tremendous to fill in the gaps visually One publishes a Mongozi speech comment on the cistern prisons and that "Listen to the end and draw the conclusion yourself. Let's accept that some Comorians who spend without calculation only to fall into poverty overnight deserve the "cisterns" (Doudry,2017). "

Ultimately, this invites reflection on the consequences of financial irresponsibility and may prompt a discussion about personal accountability, societal values, and the role of education in promoting financial literacy. Elaniou as one of the many attempts by Comorians to discredit the revolution. To quote fully a polemic against throwing the baby out with the bathwater when it comes to anti-revolutionary writing on cisterns:

> "Ali Soilih or Independence in the Cistern" is subject to caution: the grandiloquence of the tone tainted with contempt, the preposterous and outrageous nicknames bordering on slander and defamation decked out to those who have the bad idea of belonging to the wrong camp (that of Ali Soilihi), truncated words taken out of context, diverted from their meaning, false semantic studies, specious comments, cookie-cutter formulas…everything is put to use to always push further, everything that directly or indirectly affects the hated regime (Elaniou,2006, para 56). "

This warns readers to approach "Ali Soilih or Independence in the Cistern" with skepticism due to its potentially biased and manipulative nature. It suggests that the work may be driven by an agenda to discredit or undermine the regime associated with Ali Soilihi rather than providing a balanced and objective analysis. Youssouf Saïd Soilih and El Mamoun Mohamed Nassu counters Elaniou by calling it "good fiction" regarding sources and the balance sheet of the revolution:

> "Elaniou and read it as good fiction to pass the time, but in no way to learn anything either which holds the road on the Ali Soilih period. As for the debate on this period, it has been open for a long time, and the first page of the regime's balance sheet has already been written objectively, from sources that could not be more reliable, nourished by research work, investigations, and inquiries by, among others (Youssouf Saïd Soilih & El Mamoun Mohamed Nassur, year unknown).

This expresses skepticism about its historical accuracy or educational value, or as we have learned so far, both polyphonically. In the end, "Efforts to erase the traces of his passage have only partially succeeded: Ali Soilihi did not leave only the use of cisterns as prisons as a legacy (Walker, 2019, p. 67)."

Soilihi's legacy is therefore multifaceted, though weighed more toward the positive than the negative. His efforts to modernize and uplift Comorian society—through education, agrarian reform, and a bold reimagining of national identity—remain vital reference points for any emancipatory politics in the archipelago. While some critics frame his presidency in terms of "enlightened despotism," such characterizations often obscure the fact that his leadership arose from and was directed toward the people's material and cultural liberation. To reduce Soilihi merely to the trope of a benevolent autocrat is to flatten the revolutionary dynamism of his project and to deny Comorians the fullness of their socialist heritage.

Comorian-born rapper Jack L' Atout recorded the powerful track "Ali Soilih Tribute." The song stands as a cultural intervention, weaving together the themes of French class oppression, the revolutionary vision of Soilihi, and the necessity of preserving collective memory for younger generations. In its rhythms and verses, the piece becomes more than homage—it is an act of resistance, keeping alive the unfinished project of liberation and affirming the enduring relevance of Soilihi's socialist legacy in the face of ongoing neocolonial domination.

"I come to tell you that by taking independencethe Comoros had nothing, but we took the chanceI come to remind you that France, irritated by the speedof the taking of independence launches into threats,overwhelmed by events they don't know what to doand react with anger by deciding to monopolize Mayotte under their management. A chance, a liberation, Ali Soilih takes the reign of the nation mission.

n°1: Install a state of revolution.

n°2: Organization of the newly independent Comoros nation.

Ali Soilih in an emergency tries to recover Mayotte our sister island, but the resentment of the whites is too strong inside the free Comoros, Ali Soilih sets up his regime for Anjouan, Moheli and Ngazidja, action reorganization of social life, finished the colonial era in the population, each his participation, each his contribution everywhere in the regions we install the communes, everyone works for the common good, awareness of an entire nation, hard work as the only option in two months Ali Soilih has done more than during one hundred years of colonization it's true the settlers, they set up their schools, taught us their culture, their civilization, it's good but they're clever, these people they never taught us how to run our nation.

Ali Soilih knew that to combat the illusions of colonization, it was going to be hot but he didn't leave concrete until they killed him because he understood that the Comoros were as gold and as dead Babylon tried to make Ali Soilih swallow the pill, but he refused, he said no to neo colonization, no to corruption, no to medieval traditions that's why they killed him because he had taken a position on the good side. They've killed Ali Soilih but can't kill the revolution. They killed Ali Soilih but cannot kill the revolution…. etched in history as a guide…. (L'autout, muzdalifahouse.com)."

Regardless of the myths, Ali Soilihi deserves a place along with other pan-African socialist and revolutionary leaders historically and in the future. Roinak (2020) writes that "from Kwame Nkrumah to Julius Nyerere, passing by Ahmed Sékouré, Patrice Lumumba, Thomas Sankara, the former Comorian president, the Mongozi Ali Soilihi has found his place in this reduced square of the first continental pan-Africanists" (first para).

Describing the Mongozi as a "man, a man always faithful to his principles, was in the application of what he believed to be his vision on Pan-Africanism and Afrocentricity" (Roink, 2020, para 5). By characterizing Mongozi in this way, it implies that he was unwavering in his support for these ideologies and likely dedicated his life to advancing their principles.

This portrayal suggests a figure who is deeply committed to his convictions and who actively works towards realizing his vision for Africa and its diaspora. In the end, you have killed Soilihi, but like Fred Hampton, you cannot kill a revolution.

Youssouf Saïd, also a former member of the National Revolutionary Committee, later a Vice-President of the Assembly of the Union of the Comoros writes upon the cause of effects of socialism not being entrenched in Comoros. Because "[t]oday we still suffer from economic, geographical, and social imbalances. He (Soilihi) sought to create balance, to change the nature of our exchanges with the outside world and to increase internal exchanges (Giachinino,2005a, para 5)."

Lastly, as a tribute to Comorian socialism and Ali Soilihi, I will leave you with a quote by Mohamed Dossar-a former member of People's National Committee, explains the final need for a rebirth of socialism on the archipelago: "[m]any people realize that there was then a social project and a mobilization around this project…. "Now the project is what the World Bank wants to do (Giachino,2005a, para 4)."

Theory of Soilihism

Soilihism as a theory is forever connected with the Comoros. The dialectics of class struggle does not dimmish with the death of Ali Soilihi. Solihism as a force is synonymous with socialism, revolution, and independence. Yet, at the same time, Comorian socialists do not seem to agree on the very definition of Soilihist ideology. Ankili (2019) writes on how Soilihism or soolihism's meaning is ambivalent:

> "[t]oday, the name of the son Mtsashiwa (Author's note: Ali Soilihi) slams and challenges immediately in a Comorian story full of sound and fury. Ali Soilih evokes another political imagination. Against the current of the known political regimes of the Comorians, until then. Public opinion speaks of soolihism as a singular movement. On several levels, knowing that this period of history continues to divide Comorians in its apprehension (Ankili,2019, paragraph, 7).

The mention of "soolihism" as a singular movement suggests that Soilihi's tenure as president was distinctive and perhaps transformative in some way. It implies that his leadership had a significant impact on Comorian society and politics, shaping the country's trajectory in a unique manner. Soilihi had many papers and notes as guidebooks on how to infuse revolutionary ideology and praxis. These papers would have notes and invaluable polemics regarding Comorian socialism. These priceless notes of Soilihi's thoughts that would have helped creating unified theory are gone because "everything was stolen and taken away by the mercenaries in 1978 (Belletan, interview 2022)."

Soilihist Theory is based on five pillars of Marx, Lenin, Mao, Muhammed, and Rene Dumont. Dumont was a famous sociologist and agronomist that Soilihi met in Paris during his studies. Dumont is famous for authoring many books on anti-colonization that must have affected Soilihi greatly as a fellow agronomist. Regarding Muhammed and Islam, even though Soilihi denounced organized Islam, he never renounced his faith in and its need for organization. Like many liberation fighters, Soilihi was influenced by Marxism, Leninism, Maoism, and anti-colonialism events around the world.

"Soolihism is found for its part in each of these theoretical approaches and is formalized in a political imagination appealing to developmentalism. He is then distinguished by his ability to break with everyday life in his rejection of the dominant society (Ankili,2019, para7)."

Soolihism or Soilihism, is characterized by a commitment to developmentalism and a rejection of the status quo, making him a significant and distinctive figure within Comorian political thought. Many Comorians will consider Soilihism as something *sui generis* within the anticapitalist theoretical spectrum. History will be taken upon the revolutionary generations to learn " the Soilihist strategy can only be applied through a federative movement clearly committed to fighting for the sovereignty of the people, the territorial integrity and the development of the country by integrating the limits of the time and the chance of becoming (comoros-us.com)."

Soilihism is a pragmatic and action-oriented approach to governance that prioritizes the interests and well-being of the people, while also addressing broader issues of national sovereignty and development.

Unlike many other tenets of Marxist-Leninism, Mao, and Marxism, Soilihism does not emphasis the need for a vanguard party. There would be little doubt that a vanguard party would have any effect or need since the mourdiyas, the Moissy, and leadership of Ali Soilihi were the many tools of state control. The following sentence sums Soilihism:

"The leader who has the unfailing conviction that history is his only judge and who also knows that two leaders who do not agree on the path of revolution cannot both be right at the same time, there is one who can be right, the other must depart. Two men cannot be right at the same time.... Revolutionary politics does not work like that. Whoever is right being right all along the line, all reflection on the functioning of human societies shows that it is not monism from a single point of view but the pluralism of opinions that gives value to human communities and enables their progress.

Only this political pluralism establishes the dignity of citizens and respect for the rights of others. It is very surprising for a Marxist not to recognize in the dialectical process the collective elaboration of truth. A great politician once said that out of ten errors in politics, there are nine which consist in still believing true what has ceased to be so. a single point of view but the pluralism of opinions which gives value to human communities and enables their progress. Only this political pluralism establishes the dignity of citizens and respect for the rights of others. It is very surprising for a Marxist not to recognize in the dialectical process the collective elaboration of truth. A great politician once said that out of ten errors in politics, there are nine which consist in still believing true what has ceased to be so. a single point of view but the pluralism of opinions which gives value to human communities and enables their progress. Only this political pluralism establishes the dignity of citizens and respect for the rights of others. It is very surprising for a Marxist not to recognize in the dialectical process the collective elaboration of truth. It is first of all a set of errors of theoretical appreciation on the objective constraints and the conditions of possibility of introduction of socialism in an insular, agrarian, and Muslim country. And then, the political

> conviction that a very determined minority can radically change the economic and cultural foundations of a society. But that has been the zeitgeist. ... (Kweli, 2018, para, 5)."

Overall, the passage advocates for a leadership approach that values pluralism, recognizes the evolving nature of truth, and remains cognizant of historical judgment and contextual constraints.

Continuing the concept of oratory, knowledge of oral tradition and knowledge-building of which Soilihism was communicated through, Ali Soilihi seemed to tap into the sorcery/ dialectic that people needed. To have dialectics palatable and understood in the differences of witchcraft and science, Soilihist polemics describes bodily structure and biology in a complex metaphor regarding human brain, blood circulation, and automobile working. Soilihi (Lafon, 1991) "started from the principle that everything, without exception, from politics to Marxist dialectics, from religion to economic program or agronomy, could and should be expressed in Comorian (p. 45)."

Ali Soilihi was comfortable in either in dashiki or in jeans and used his almost imagist magi-visage to persuade the masses on their terms. By adapting his appearance and style, Soilihi and Soilihism were able to speak to the masses in a way that resonated with them. This suggests a keen understanding of his audience and an ability to communicate in a manner that made his message accessible and compelling.

Furthermore, as Lafon (1991) suggests that: "Ali Soilih often proceeded by images, by comparisons and by repetitions (...) [to] better understand a new expression to a popular public that could disconcert lexical innovations and a conceptualization which, wanting to be scientific, reproduced a foreign classification (Lafon,1991, p. 34)."

Soilihi was mindful of the need to communicate in a way that resonated with his audience. He likely avoided using overly technical or foreign language that could alienate or confuse his listeners. Instead, he opted for more straightforward and familiar language to ensure that his messages were easily understood.

As part of theoretical dialectics, theory is a way to describe things. It is praxis that lets us as revolutionaries figure out if a political theory has merit. Yet, theory and philosophy are a way to make connections, previous connections were not made before. As above, Soilihism as a very pluralistic mindset. Regarding three years of Soilihism, the conscious will to demolish feudal and outdated forms of feudalism, patriarchy, and conservative oppression was very real in exploring more bounds.

Finally, the important last words of Ali Soilihi and his foundation of theoretical legacy is the overall takeaway from Soilihism:

> "The day after his assassination, some of his early companions explained with great euphemisms their organized surrender. It is the guide himself, who would have encouraged them to lay down their arms to avoid a bloodbath for the people. He would have predicted his death, adding: 'if I am arrested, give up the fight, and if I am

> missed, follow my steps (Giachino, 2018, para 6)."

This beautifully captures the tumultuous journey of the Comorian people towards independence and their subsequent experiment with socialism. It highlights the resilience and determination of a nation striving for self-determination and social justice, despite facing numerous challenges and setbacks along the way.

The mention of Ali Soilihi as a visionary leader underscores the importance of leadership in driving transformative change, while also acknowledging the complexities and contradictions inherent in implementing socialist ideals in a real-world context. The narrative effectively portrays the idealism and pragmatism that often coexist in revolutionary movements, as well as the external forces that can both support and undermine such endeavors.

Overall, this work tried to capture the spirit of resilience, solidarity, and hope that characterizes the struggle for social justice around the world, making it a powerful testament to the human capacity for change and transformation.

By emphasizing the enduring legacy of Comorian socialism, the narrative encourages reflection on the broader struggle for freedom and justice, serving as a source of inspiration for future generations.

It calls for a reexamination of history to challenge dominant narratives and envision alternative paths towards liberation and equality.

As Marxists and revolutionaries, we will never know the "perfect" step or conditions of when we can go on creating on 1, 2,3, new Social and Secular Republics. Soilihi using Soilihism knew that through revolution and the break of the past, that Comorian identity have the ability to control their destiny. The epitome of what a revolutionary socialist for self-determination of the country from the fetters of colonization, feudalism, and capitalism should advocated during a revolutionary situation. In the end the revolution, Soilihism as a "revolution du verbe" left imprints on people's memories. Contemporary international anti-imperialist activists in Comoros continue to use the slogan "Another world is possible" to continue to seek ideas and themselves in Soilihism.

Short Epilogue: Maore/Mayotte

Over the years, a series of French leaders exchanged short-term electoral gains for department status of the island. Maore/Mayotte is to be a particular item on the agenda of the National Assembly. Almost every year there are referendums on how to proceed with the island's status. These are only pittance to make France be seen more favorable with its depiction as a democratic state towards its overseas neo-colonial empire. The Comoros continues to claim the island, while criticizing the French military base and occupation. Lately, French deputy and senator from the French Communist Party declares that the French parliament that French activity in Maore are a criminal endeavor. Giving praise to the PCF, Abdou Ahmad writes that "w]e just want to salute the constancy of the PCF for forty-five years in its commitment against the balkanization of the Comoros by the French state (Ahmad 2020, para 6)." Echoing Abdou Ahmad, **as** anti-imperialist revolutionaries we need to add to our grocery list of the demands whether immediate and transition that Comoros has the right to unification with Maroe!

Appendix A

Figure 1. Stamps from the Social and Secular Republic of Comoros using the official socialist flag

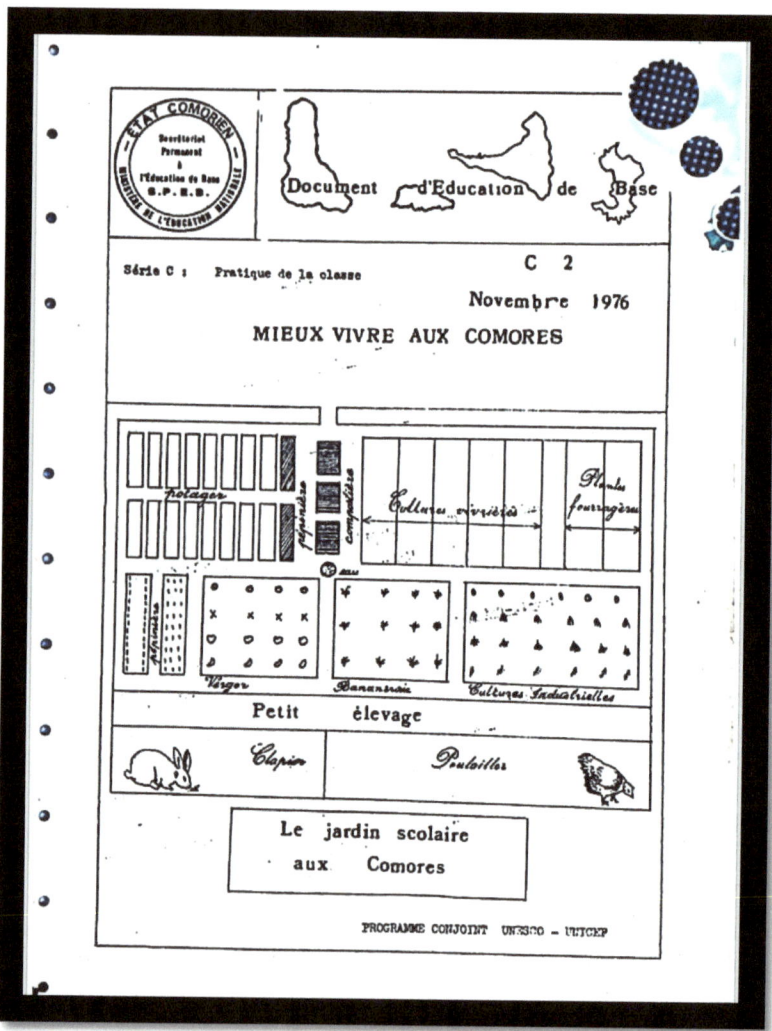

Figure 2. Blueprint for a school garden in Comoros. The top caption reads in French "A Better Life in Comoros"

Figure 3. Contemporary abstract painting with "mapinduzi" or revolutionaries with Comroian kids and early picture of Ali Soilhi

Figure 4. Contemporary African-style picture of Ali Soilhi

Figure 5. Ali Soilihi date unknown

Figure 6. Grave of Ali Soilihi

Figure 7. Official flag of the Social and Secular Republic of Comoros 1975-1978

Appendix B: Constitution of the Social and Secular Republic of Comoros

1. Preamble.

   The Comorian people proclaim:

   - its determination to liberate by all means the island of Mahoré, an integral part of its territory illegally occupied by France.
   - its solidarity with all people in the fight against racism and domination:
   - its attachment to the authentic values of the Islamic religion. Values which, among others, involve the fight against the exploitation of ignorance and credulity, through charlatanism and idleness.
   - its attachment to all the principles of the Universal Declaration of Human Rights adopted by the United Nations on December 10, 1948.
   - work is a right and an obligation for all those, men and women who are not prevented by age or physical incapacity. The State therefore strives to promote full employment and to assure everyone fair remuneration for their participation in production.
   - In respect of the natural balances which condition their renewal, all the natural resources of the Comoros, soils, subsoils, forests, maritime waters,

and seabed, must be exploited in the best interest is general. _ _ _ Property rights cannot in any way obstruct this necessity; _

- Equality of rights between men and women is understood both on the civil and civic level as well as on the effective level of employment and promotion possibilities.
- The Administration serves manual workers and remains under their control. The cost of its operation inevitably comes as a deduction from the share of budgetary revenues intended for productive investments, it must be kept to a minimum.
- The Administration only provides essential services which cannot yet be provided by manual workers themselves. Training for young people and adults is designed to guide all communities towards self-management.

2. Title one.

Sovereignty. _

First article.

The Comoros archipelago is one and indivisible. It constitutes a Secular and Social Democratic Republic. The State is the instrument of manual workers to improve their living conditions.

The territory of the Comorian Republic includes four islands:

- Mahor é (Mayotte)
- Ndzwani (Anjouan)
- Mwali (Moh é li)
- Ngazidja (Grande Comore)

Article 2.

> The Comorian State ensures the equality of all citizens before the law, without distinction of origin, race, religious or philosophical conviction.

Article 3.

> The national emblem is the red and green flag, the lower third of which is green. In the red surface, which occupies the upper two-thirds, a white crescent and four white diamond-shaped stars are inscribed from the shaft.
>
> The national anthem is: COMOR MASIWA MANE.
>
> The motto is "Work – Unity – Progress".

Article 4.

> The principle of the Comorian Republic is local power, which means that the political and administrative organization allows each community to decide for itself the financial and material means corresponding to these questions.
>
> Administrative bodies only deal with issues of common interest for the entire population of the archipelago and respect the management autonomy of the various local and regional authorities. regional. _

Article 5.

> National sovereignty belongs to the people who exercise it through direct and indirect suffrage.

Voters are all citizens of both sexes aged at least 15 years, who enjoy their civil rights.

The civil and criminal majority will be defined by order.

Article 6.

Youth and more particularly student youth are the spearhead of popular entertainment.

Living in symbiosis with manual workers, she is constantly immersed in social practice.

It introduces workers to the scientific understanding of technical questions and develops criticism of traditional methods.

Article 7.

The People's Army ensures the defense of the territory and vanguard of the workers; it protects revolutionary gains.

Through its active participation in national production the army remains an army of workers, and it tends towards economic self-sufficiency.

3. Title II.

Territorial constituencies.

Article 8.

The national territory is divided into bavous.

Each bayou has management autonomy and is administered by a Liwali.

Article 9.

> The Bavous administration is in direct contact with the Council of State.

Article 10.

> The number and limits of the bavous are defined by ordinance.

Article 11.

> Each island constitutes a Wilaya placed under the authority of a Mouhafidh elected by indirect universal suffrage.

Article 12.

> Each bavou is divided into mouridayas, which bring together a certain number of villages and a population of between 3,000 and 6,000 inhabitants.
>
> The mouridayas are administered by a Mounir.
>
> The number and limitations of the mouridayas, are specified by ordinance.

4. Title III.

The authorities of popular power.

Section 13.

> The Comorian people organize themselves at the level of villages, city neighborhoods, mouridayas, wilayas, places of work or study and at the national level, in popular committees.

Section 14.

    The basic popular committees, which is to say the village and neighborhood committees, are elected by direct universal suffrage and by list ballot, the modalities of this ballot being precise e es by prescription.

Article 15.

    The popular committees of the mouridayas, emanate from the grassroots popular committees.

Section 16.

    The popular committees of mouridayas meet periodically in bavou congresses.

Section 17.

    The popular committees of the wilayas emanate from the popular committees of the mouridayas,

    The popular committee of each wilaya elects the Mouhafidh.

Section 18.

    The National Popular Committee also emanates from the popular committees of mouridayas,

    The National People's Committee meets in ordinary session on the first Monday of each quarter. The normal duration of the session is three days.

Section 19.

> The popular committees renew their office every year.

Article 20.

> The national congress is the supreme body of Popular Power.
>
> It is constituted by the meeting of all the members of the Moudiyas committees.
>
> He proposes the candidates for the Presidency and the Vice- President of the Council of State.

Article 21.

> The bodies of Popular Power are associated by the Council of State with the treatment of all the following questions:
>
> ➢ Planning,
> ➢ Defense and security, _ _
> ➢ Information,
> ➢ Youth and sports,
> ➢ Cultural and artistic affairs.
>
> The precise limitations of the respective powers of Popular Power and the Council of State will be specified by ordinance.

5. Title IV.

> The state Council.

Section 22.

> Subject to the provisions of the first paragraph of article 46 below, the President and the Vice- President of the Council of

State are elected together. by direct universal suffrage by majority vote in two rounds for five years.

Section 23.

The President of the Council of State bears the title of President of the Comorian Republic. He is the Head of State.

It ensures compliance with the Basic Law and its preamble. It ensures the regular functioning of public authorities and the continuity of the State.

It is the guarantor of the integrity of the national territory, independence and national security and respect for international commitments.

Section 24.

The Council of State includes, in addition to its President and Vice-President, a maximum of 9 members appointed and dismissed by the President after consultation with the National People's Committee.

Article 25.

The Council of State, based on the political directives adopted by the National Congress, defines, and conducts the policy of the Nation.

It has the Army, the Administration and in particular the National Planning-Methods - Finance Center. It ensures the execution of the legislation in force. He exercises regulatory power.

Article 26.

A portion of the members of the Council of State designated by the President of this Council constitutes the Central Committee of Internal Affairs.

Section 27.

of the Council of State designated by the President of this Council constitutes the Central Committee for External Affairs.

Section 28.

The Coordinator of the Central Committee for Internal Affairs bears the title of Minister of State for Internal Affairs.

The Coordinator of the Central Committee for External Affairs bears the title of Minister of State for External Relations.

Within each of the two central committees, decisions are taken in a collegial manner.

Section 29.

In association with the National People's Committee, the State Council exercises legislative power. The President of the Republic signs the ordinances, decrees and orders adopted by this Council.

Article 30.

The President of the Republic appoints people to civil and military positions in the State.

He exercises the right of pardon after consultation with the Supreme Court.

It accredits ambassadors and extraordinary envoys to foreign powers. _

Ambassadors and extraordinary foreign envoys are accredited to him. _

Section 31.

In the event of a vacancy in the presidency of the Council of State or an impediment noted by the majority of the members making up this Council, the functions of Head of State are carried out by the Vice- President, and if he is in turn prevented from exercising these functions, by the Coordinator of the Central Committee of Internal Affairs.

When the impediment of the President is declared definitive by the National People's Committee, its coordinator convenes the congress and organizes the election of the new President and a Vice -President resident, thirty days at most after the declaration of the definitive nature of the impediment.

Section 32.

State institutions, national territorial integrity, the independence of the Nation and the execution of its international commitments are threatened, and the regular functioning of public authorities is compromise, the President of the State Council takes the decisions required by the circumstances, after consultation with the permanent office of the National People's Committee.

These decisions aim to ensure that constitutional public authorities, as quickly as possible, have the means to normally accomplish their mission.

He informs the Nation of these decisions by messages.

Section 33.

matters must be the subject of an order:

- civil rights and fundamental guarantees granted to citizens for the exercise of public freedoms.
- The constraints imposed by National Security on citizens in their person and their property.
- The state and capacity of people, the matrimonial regime, inheritance, liberalities.
- The determination of crimes and offenses and the penalties applicable to them.
- The creation and organization of jurisdictional orders.
- Amnesty.
- The base, the rate, the methods of recovery of taxes and charges of all kinds.
- The determination of State resources and expenses.
- The currency issue regime
- The creation of public establishments.
- The determination of the fundamental principles of administration.
- The general principles of teaching.
- Social law.
- Membership in international organizations.

Section 34.

> The National People's Committee is associated with the development of draft ordinances by the Council of State.

6. Title V.

　International treaties and agreements.

Section 35.

> The President of the Council of State negotiates and ratifies the treaties. It is informed of any negotiations aimed at the conclusion of an international agreement not subject to ratification.

Section 36.

> Treaties or agreements regularly ratified or approved have, from their publication, an authority greater than that of the laws, subject for each agreement or treaty to its application by the other party.
>
> Any international commitment containing a clause contrary to the Basic Law can only be ratified or approved after the revision of the Basic Law by an extraordinary national congress.

7. Title VI.

　The judicial authority.

Section 3.

> The President of the Council of State guarantees the independence of justice.

Section 38.

> The judicial organization includes a Court of First Instance in each moudiria. a Court of Appeal in each bavou and a national Supreme Court.

Section 39.

> In case of high treason or forfeiture. The President of the Council of State is indicted by the National People's Committee and tried by the National Congress in an Extraordinary People's Court.

8. Title VII.

Comorian nationality.

Article 40.

> Any person born to one or more parents of Comorian nationality has the right to Comorian nationality.

Article 41.

> The Council of State can grant Comorian nationality.

Section 42.

> Comorians residing abroad, whatever their nationality, may be represented in the National Popular Committee and the National Congress by observers appointed by the Council of State.

9, Title VIII.

>The revision.

>Section 43.

>>The initiative for revising the Basic Law belongs to the Council of State.

>>revision projects are submitted to the National Congress assembled in session in extraordinary session by the Council of State.

>>No review procedure may be initiated or pursued when its purpose or consequence would be to undermine the integrity of the national territory.

>Section 44.

>>republican form of the State cannot be subject to revision.

10. Title IX.

>Transitional provisions.

>Section 45.

>>The State institutions provided for by this Basic Law will be put in place within a period of six months from the date of its promulgation are responsible for setting up the new institutions.

>>The Moudirs will be designated by the Council of State until the liberation of Mahoré. An order will then specify the terms of their election.

Section 46.

Until the liberation of the Comorian island of Mahoré, the President and the Vice- President were elected by the Congress.

A referendum will be organized after the release of Mahoré to ratify this Basic Law.

Appendix C: Snippets from the Documentary La Reform Araire by Bambao Radio Télévision (BRTV)

Figure 1.

Figure 2.

Figure 3.

Figure 4.

Figure 5.

Dietsche

Figure 6.

Bibliography

Abdou, A. (2020) This July 6 without drums. MuzdalifaHouse.com Retrieved from https://muzdalifahouse.com/2020/07/06/encore-un-6-juillet-sans-tambours/"

Arm, (19, August 2019). Ali Soilih: It was 3 August, 44 years ago. Lemohoelien. Retrieved from (http://lemohelien.com/ali-Soilih-cetait-le-3-aout-1975-il-y-a-donc-44-ans)

Abdoul-Djabar, N. and Zakaria, Y. (2/6/2/2021). Radio under the Soolihist revolution. From 1976 to 1978 I A multifunctional tool for the government Al-Watwan. Retrieved from https://alwatwan.net/societe/la-radio-sous-la-r%C3%A9volution-Soilihste.-1976-%C3%A0-1978-i-un-outil-multifonctionnel-pour-le-gouvernement.html 2/6/21

Ankili, H. (2019, May 29) In Memory of the Mongozi. Muzalifa House. Retrieved from (https://muzdalifahouse.com/2019/05/29/7695/).

Alemayehu, Iyasou (2020, September,9) The Struggle for Democracy in Africa. https://cosmonaut.blog /2020/09/09/the-struggle-for-democracy-in-africa-by-iyasou-alemayehu/ b

Bambao-RTV Mvouni-Bambao (2015). Ali Soilih Mtsachiwa _ la révolution comorienne de 1975 [Video]. [YouTube.] Retrieved. https://www.youtube.com/watch?v=3DGOud-w3MM&t=197s

Bakar, Abdourahim Saïd (1988). "Small Island Systems: A Case Study of the Comoro Islands." Comparative Education 24, no. 2 181–91. http://www.jstor.org/stable/3099074.

Bellantan, L (2022) private email. 2 February 2022.

BioGreat Tv 2021 YouTube "Biography of Ali Soilih M'tsashiwa" https://www.youtube.com/watch?v=1Uc0AIc4hqM&t=278 s.).

Biel, R (2015). "Eurocentrism and the Communist Movement". Kersplebedeb. Montreal, Quebec.

"Biography of Ali Soilih M'tsashiwa" "Biography of Ali Soilih M'tsashiwa [Video]. (YouTube). Retrieved from https://www.youtube.com/watch?v=1Uc0AIc4hqM&t=278 s.).

BlogAfrica4. Retrieved 1/30/24. https://www.liberation.fr/dossier/blog-africa4/

Chife, A. (1997). "The Political Economy of Post-Cold War Africa" (NY: Edwin Mellon Press)

Clancy, T (2014) ... Union of the Comoros.

Comoroes-Online.com Retrieved from (http://www.comores-online.com/mwezinet/histoire/Soilih.htm).

Country Studies Comores Retrieved from http://countrystudies.us/comoros/5.htm

Damir Ben Ali (2009) Soilhi and Radio. Ali Al-Watwan. Retried from https://alwatwan.net/societe/damir-ben-ali,-historien-%C2%ABla-radio-a-permis-%C3%A0-ali-Soilih-de-pr%C3%A9parer-les-esprits%C2%BB.html

Daou, Nicholas A., "Constitutional Reform: Decolonization in the Comoros Islands" (2017). Capstone Collection. 3065.

Retried from
https://digitalcollections.sit.edu/capstones/3065

Denard, B (no year) orbspatrianostria.com

Documents Officiels. (1979). United States: UN.

Dododry. (2014). Ali Soilih Mtsachioi discours sur divers points qui sont actuellement à jour en France. [Video]. [YouTube. Retrieved from. https://www.youtube.com/watch?v=cXuzuxP9lzo)."

Djimbo la Komori. (2020, June5). Komori. [Video]. YouTube. https://www.youtube.com/watch?v=5D4cw50cdMo

Doury (2017). Ali Soilih Anda. [Video]. [YouTube.] Retrieved. https://www.youtube.com/watch?v=LKz8Gm44Gb4

Elbadawi, S (2005, April 4). Ali Soilhi: Maker of Imagination. Muzdalifa House. Retrieved from https://muzdalifahouse.com/2005/04/04/ali-Soilih-fabricant-dimaginaire/

Enemies of the Father Land (2017, April 6). Personne n'a choisi ses parents' par Président Ali Soilih [Video]. [YouTube]. https://www.youtube.com/watch?v=SjAAQlqN8xY&t=30s

Fanon, F. (1967). *The Wretched of the Earth.* Grove Press. New York...

Favoreu, L., & Maestre, J. C. (1975). L'accession des Comores à l'indépendance. Annuaire des pays de l'Océan Indien, 2, 15-33.

French, Howard. "The Mercenary Position." Transition, no. 73, 1997, pp. 110–21, https://doi.org/10.2307/2935448. Accessed 2 May 2022.

Fondation Matschima, (2022). Retrieved from https://www.facebook.com/FondationMtsachiya

Fondation Mtsachiya (2018, October) Ali Soilih Mtsachiwa et la révolution 1975-78[Video]. [YouTube]. https://www.youtube.com/watch?v=0bXUF3Q9Jqg

Giachino, L (2021, October,25) Bob Denard in the Comros or the Reign of the 'Angels" Mudalifa House Retrieved from"https://muzdalifahouse.com/2021/10/25/bob-denard-aux-comores-ou-le-regne-des-anges/

Giachino, L (2018, May 29). Zapara Mongzonzi Zitso Hupara. Muzdalifa House Retrieved from https://muzdalifahouse.com/2018/05/29/zapara-mongozi-zitso-hupara/.

Giancho, L. (2005a, April 4). Ali Soilhi a President too soon. Muzdalifa House. Retrieved from https://muzdalifahouse.com/2005/04/04/ali-Soilih-un-president-venir-trop-tot/

Giancho, L. (2005b, April 4). Land of the Beardless Muzdalifa House Retrieved from. https://muzdalifahouse.com/2005/04/04/lepopee-des-imberbes/

Giachino, L (2005c, April 4). The Hard Way According to Soilhi. Muzdalifa House Retrieved from https://muzdalifahouse.com/2005/04/04/la-maniere-forte-selon-Soilih/

Giachino, L (20005d, April 4) Ali Soilhi Misunderstood Visionary. Retrieved from https://muzdalifahouse.com/2005/04/04/ali-Soilih-visionnaire-incompris/

Habriza Comroes (2015, January,). Le President Ali Soilhi mtaschinwa ou. Retrieved.

https://www.habarizacomores.com/2015/01/le-president-ali-Soilih-mtsachiwa-ou.html

Habriza Comroes (2020, May.), eclairage Ali Soilhi netait pas. Retrieved from https://www.habarizacomores.com/2020/05/eclairage-ali-Soilih-netait-pas.html?m=1&fbclid=IwAR0xqCY7aAh5CoSGRKFIIkpVmVpkXiyDLmCsGePjTklSO1XvJp4JKwgiwOc

Hugounenc, P. (2022" Bob Denard: The Story of a Man. Paris. Phillipe Hugonenc

Hebditch, D. & Connor, K. (2017) How to stage a military coup. Skyhourse Publishing. New York

Horst, I.S. (2020). Like Ho Chi Minh! Like Che Guevara!: The Revolutionary Left in Eithiopia,1969-1979. Paris. *Foreign Language Press*.

Kaka, A. (2017). Comoros Economy and Political Leadership: Comoros's General Administrative Outline. (n.p.): CreateSpace Independent Publishing Platform.

Kweli, K. (2018, February,5) Muzdalifa House. https://muzdalifahouse.com/2018/02/05/5831

Keri, K. (2024) Private email.

Lamb, D (1982). "*The Africans.*" Random House. New York.

Lenin, V. (1917) Meeting of The All-Russia Central Executive Committee. Retrieved from marxists.org

November 4 (17), 1917

Lafon, M. (1991). Lexique Français-Comorien (Shingazidja). Paris: L'Harmatta.

La Gazette Des Comores (May 3, 1978). Retrieved from https://lagazettedescomores-com.translate.goog/culture/litt%C3%A9rature-/-sortied%E2%80%99un-livre-bibliographique-sur-l%E2%80%99%C3%A9poque-Soilihste-.html?_x_tr_sl=fr&_x_tr_tl=en&_x_tr_hl=en&_x_tr_pto=sc

Marxists.org Retrieved from https://www.marxists.org/subject/china/peking-review/1976/PR1976-49.pdf)

Mao, Z. (1961). Selected works of Mao Tse-Tung. Oxford: Distributed throughout the world by Pergamon Press.

(Marx, K (1867). Capital, Chapter Thirty-one Genesis of the Industrial Capitalist. Retrieved from Marxists.org

Mawana Afrobeat (2018). Mawana Afrobeat - MOUDIRYA (tribute to Ali Soilih) [YouTube]. [Video.' Retrieved at https://www.youtube.com/watch?v=mV4ZQNHcnGQ"

Mawasai, (May 29,1978 The Death of Ali Soilihi). 4 June 2023. Ed. 432. Retrieved from https://masiwa-comores.com/politique/29-mai-1978-la-mort-dali-soilihi/

Mouvement Comorien des Jeunes Soilihistes (2017). Retrieved from https://www.facebook.com/profile.php?id=100068959488110&sk=about

Mukonoweshuro, E. G. (1990). The Politics of Squalor and Dependency: Chronic Political Instability and Economic Collapse in the Comoro Islands. African Affairs, 89 (357), 555–577. http://www.jstor.org/stable/722174

Muzdalifa House (2005, April 4) Founding Father. https://muzdalifahouse.com/2005/04/04/pere-fondateur/

Muzdalifa House, (2023, January 6). Muzdalifa House. Retrieved, from https://muzdalifahouse.com/

Niza, Ali Mohamed di (1976) Peking Review. Retrieved from https://www.marxists.org/subject/china/peking-review/1982/PR1982-11.pdf"

North Korea Quarterly (1977). Vol. 10–13. Institute of Asian Affairs... p. 5

Nationale Soilihste Generation https://www.facebook.com/profile.php?id=100049613658093

Oboyo-ombo Pioneers, Rebels, and a few Villains 150 Years of Journalism in Eastern Africa KAS Media Programme Sub-Sahara Africa Republic of South Africa www.kas.de/mediaafrica

Ottenheimer, H (1985). Marriage in Domoni.Salem, WI. Sheffield Publishing Company.

Ottenheimer, H., Ottenheimer, M. (1994A). Historical dictionary of the Comoro Islands. United Kingdom: Scarecrow Press.

Patrimmonie, S. (2022, May 27). Muzdalifa House.

Peterson, B. J. (2021). Thomas Sankara: A Revolutionary in Cold War Africa. Bloomington. Indiana University Press.

Roinaka (05 February 2020) Panafricanisme: Mongozi Ali Soilih ne fut-il pas le 1er Panafricaniste comorien. Retrieved https://roinaka.skyrock.com/3329910960-Panafricanisme-Mongozi-Ali-Soilih-ne-fut-il-pas-le-1er-Panafricaniste.html

Rijke-Epstein, T. (2017). Architectures of Belonging: Moral Economies of Urban Place-Making in Mahajanga, Madagascar.

Rodney, W. (1972). *How Europe underdeveloped Africa.* London: Bogle-L'Ouverture Publications.

Sankara, T (1984), United Nations General Assembly Official Records, 20th Plenary Meeting, Thursday, 4 October 1984, at 10.40 a.m., New York, (A/39/PV.20), pp. 405-410.

Saindou, Kamal 'Eddine (2021, December,3). December 1976 Majunda Massacre The Buried Truth. Muzdaifa House. Retrieved from https://muzdalifahouse.com/2021/12/03/decembre-1976-massacre-de-majunga-la-verite-enfouie/#_ftn1

Saindou, Kamal'Eddine (2022, November 4) ASEC or When Comorian Youth Dreamed of Revolution. Muzdalfia House. Retrieved from muzdalifahouse.com/2022/11/04/16560/

Saïd Soilih, Y.S. & Nassur, El Mamound (year unknown). Ali Soilih, the broken momentum? (L'Harmattan).

Terrill, W (1986). The Comoro Islands in South African Regional Strategy. Africa Today, 33(2/3), 59–70. retrieved from http://www.jstor.org/stable/4186361

Thomassankara.net" Thomas Sankara of Comoros?" Retrieved from https://www.thomassankara.net/ali-Soilih-mtsashiwa-1937-1978-le-sankara-des-comores/?fbclid=IwAR16V-WsapgBJ9IAZJcAS-EteXvD-sO9Q2JJmmuYDjUwG1XFjVgm_YAskjk

Times Magazine (1975, August,30) Comores Coup. Retrieved from. http://www.time.com/time/magazine/article/0,9171,919809,00.html#ixzz12L9LSl7y

Ufwakuzi-Revolution. Speech by President Ali Soilihi. 1975 Editions-Coelancante (2024). Retrieved on https://www.editions-coelacanthe.com/histoire

Umma Juzur lkamar (2011). [Video]. [YouTube] Retrieved from https://www.youtube.com/watch?v=hVE38vSyt-8 YouTube

Venter, D (1990)."The Comorian comitragedy: Final curtain on Abdallahism? Dr Denis Venter, Chief Researcher at the Africa Institute, looks at the circumstances surrounding the death of the Comoros President Abdallah and at the prospects facing the island republic's new government. "Africa Insight, vol 20, no 3.

Walker, I. (2007). What Came First, The Nation or the State? Political Process in the Comoros Island. Africa,77 (4), 582-605. Doi:10.3366/aft.2007.77.4.582

Walker, I. (2019). Islands in a Cosmopolitan Sea: A History of the Comoros. United Kingdom: Oxford University Press.

Weinberg S. (1994). Last of the Pirates. Pantheon books.

Wolin, R. (2018) The Wind from the East: French Intellectuals, The Cultural revolution, and the legacy of the 1960's. Princeton. Princeton University Press

Index

Abdulrahman Mohamed Babu..................42–43

African National Congress (ANC, Tanganyika)..................39

Ali Soilihi..................xvii–xix, 54–63, 74–77, 154–155

    life..................xvii–xviii, 54–63, 74–77

    death..................154–155

    coup came to power (Aug 3, 1975)..................xvii, 63

    coup overthrown (May 13, 1978)..................xvii–xviii, 154–155

    theory (Soilihism)..................189–195

Association of Students and Trainees from the Comoros in France (AESC)..................after p. 170

Bob Denard..................xiii–xv, 150–160, 154–155

Comoros (general)..................xvii–xix, 27–37, 61–63

    early history..................27–33

    independence..................33–37, 61–63

    feudalism..................27–33

    French colonial rule..................27–32

    Islam influence..................xvii–xviii

Comorian Associations (networks).........................38–39

Congress Party for the Independence of Madagascar..46

Constitution (Social and Secular Republic).......203–216

Democratic People's Republic of Korea....................134

Flag (Social and Secular Republic).......................87–89

Foundation Mtsashiwa...xii, xxii

Franz Fanon...xi–xii, xix

Grande Marriages..112

Iconi..141–146

Islands...27–33

    Ngazidja / Grande Comoros..............................27–32

    Ndzuani / Anjouan...27–32

    Mwali / Mohéli..viii

    Maore / Mayotte.......................viii, 58–61, 74–77, 195

Jean-Paul Sartre..xix

Karl Marx...x–xi, 189–195

Madagascar..45–47, 136–140

    see also Congress Party for the Independence of Madagascar

Madagascar for the Malagasy..46

Majunga Rataka..136

Mao Tse-Tung..ix

Biographies

Author

Lucas Alan Dietsche (pronouns: He, Comrade, Accomplice) is a Ph.D. student at the Institute for Doctoral Studies in Visual Arts with a master's in criminal justice from the University of Wisconsin. An eclectic researcher, his interests include the Hegelian death of art, poetry, zines, Poetic Inquiry Criminology, and carceral tourism. He was both Red Mug Coffeehouse's only Poet Laureate and Superior, Wisconsin's first. Dietsche is an adjunct professor in Adams State University's Prison Education program and a 2023–2024 Minnesota State Art Board grantee, funding projects to publish justice-impacted writings and document Indigenous and Poor Farm cemeteries.

His work explores boundaries and the concept of "(s)place," a variable occupying both space and place, drawing on theoretical, aesthetic, and poetic disciplines to develop new poetics. He critiques repetitive imagery in late-capitalist poetry and studies writers who bypass mainstream publishing to self-publish. Rejecting confessionalism and neo-impressionism, he leaves the classification of his evolving work to future literature students.

Dietsche is an editor for the Transformative Justice Journal and author of Commies and Zombies, Since the Oregon Trail, Moods are Like Wisconsin Weather, Kapshida., and For God's Throwaway Children. Inspired by Dada, surrealism, and figures such as Marcel Duchamp, Tristan Tzara, Frida Kahlo, Mina Loy, Sylvia Plath, and Hunter S. Thompson, he is also co-campaign manager for Gladis the Orca's 2024 presidential run. He can be reached at lucasdietsche81@gmail.com.

Editors

Marie Moldovan is a Saskatchewan-born, Ontario-based publisher, illustrator, and poet whose work bridges trauma and transformation. A former Canadian Forces medic and self-proclaimed "jack of many trades," Marie channels resilience and artistry into their imprint, *I Ain't Your Marionette Press*. Their debut collection, *20 Years of Winter*, blends poetry and visual art to confront service-related PTSD, grief, and survival—offering solidarity and empowerment to fellow survivors. Through creation, Marie has reclaimed narrative control and now champions voices that refuse to be silenced.

 ***Joseph Mykut*** is a multidisciplinary creator from Alabama whose work spans writing, illustration, photography, editing, and literary advocacy. Their art and photography have been exhibited internationally and featured in Canadian anthologies including *3 Amigos Ink*, *Splatter: Lonely Soul in the Darkness*, *The Way of the Crow*, and *Shattered Psyche*, all published by *I Ain't Your Marionette Press*. Joseph is also the author and illustrator of the children's books *Beautiful Boy* and *There's a Me Under My Bed*.

Rooted in the quiet magic of everyday life, Joseph's creative practice invites viewers to find beauty in the overlooked. As a two-spirited member of the LGBTQ2+ community and a practitioner of Shamanism, they explore the sacred balance between light and dark, seen and unseen. Their spiritual path—shaped in the Bible Belt and expanded through universal inquiry—guides their work as an ordained minister with the Universal Life Church. Through art and story, Joseph builds bridges between worlds, encouraging others to connect with their own truths.

Suggested Reads

The Way of the Crow Anthology

Crows are fascinating. They are intelligent creatures with a dark demeanor and an aptitude for recognizing and collecting beautiful eclectic artifacts and trinkets. This anthology, so affectionately named, has managed to honor just that, the magical way of the crow. Collected within the binds of this book is beautiful and sometimes hopeless poetry, stories, and ideas adorned with stunning images and artistry that simultaneously inspire, captivate, and even devastate the psyche of the reader. The crows of humanity have flocked together here on the pages of this masterpiece from all parts of the world, carrying with them jewels and treasures as beautiful offerings to their audience. This book is an aviary filled with poetic plumage striking enough to set flight to your senses. Sit back, open your heart and let your mind soar above the winds of imagination with the literary experience of The Way of the Crow.

Gods, Goddesses, Atheists and Such an anthology

There is something timeless about a poem. Something sacred in the stroke of a brush. Long before we built temples, we carved meaning into cave walls and bled truth into verses. Before we named gods, we sang to stars. Before we denied them, we searched for them in each other.

This anthology, Gods, Goddesses, Atheist and Such, is not a sermon. It is not a doctrine. It is a convergence, a gathering of voices from every corner of the world, each with their own lens on the divine, the disillusioned, the sacred, the skeptical, and everything in between.

Within these pages are prayers written in ink, confessions sculpted in charcoal, revelations that come not with thunder but in the soft hush of being seen. Some speak to gods with reverence. Some speak back with defiance. Others speak only to themselves, and in doing so, speak to us all.

This collection is a temple with no doors, a gallery with no gatekeeper. Every offering is welcome. Every doubt is honored. Every truth is held.

May you find yourself somewhere in this alchemy of belief and unbelief. May you feel less alone in your questions, more alive in your awe, and deeply human in your hunger for meaning.

Welcome to the space between the sacred and the shattered. Welcome to Gods, Goddesses, Atheist and Such.

www.ingramcontent.com/pod-product-compliance
Lightning Source LLC
Chambersburg PA
CBHW042055290426

44111CB00001B/11